Dedication

To all readers of Swedenborg's writings, and particularly to those of you who have been faithful readers for many years, I extend grateful appreciation for your devotion and understanding as this new poetic version becomes a reality.

Also, to my wife, Jane, who encouraged me to keep searching the writings for those special passages suitable for free-verse rendition, and without whose help this volume could not have been completed.

L.C.L.

Poems from *Swedenborg*

by Leon C. Le Van

First Printing 1987
ISBN 0-87785-134-4

Library of Congress Catalog Card Number 87-060469

Swedenborg Foundation, Inc.
139 East 23rd Street
New York, NY 10010

Manufactured in the United States of America

Preface

All the prose passages from which these poems are structured are taken verbatim from the following works by Emanuel Swedenborg: Divine Providence (P); Divine Love and Wisdom (DLW); Heaven and Its Wonders and Hell (H); Conjugial Love (CL); Apocalypse Revealed (R); Apocalypse Explained (E); Soul and Body (SB); New Jerusalem and Its Heavenly Doctrines (HD); True Christian Religion (T); and Arcana Coelestia.

The Table of Contents does not undertake to list all the poems. Rather, it lists only the lead-off poem on each page so that the page may be easily identified for ready reference.

The poems are not in sequence. They can be read with equal enjoyment wherever the book is opened. They are like the autumn leaves that fall to the ground in the only sequence that Divine Providence gives them. Each can be enjoyed wherever it is found.

This little book is not designed to be a tool for study. It is for enjoyment; for light of truth; for aid to perception; for better understanding of Heaven, hell, and angels; for fuller reception of influx from the Lord God the Savior. It testifies everywhere to the existence of the Kingdom of God and the Spiritual World.

It cannot be stated too clearly that Swedenborg did not compose any of these poems. Swedenborg did not write poetry. But at many points in his monumental writings there is rhythm and cadence. Many passages show more notable rhythm and cadence, for example, than is found in some poems by Robert Browning. Based on that fact I have constructed the poems in the following free-verse manner. I tremble at the results but humbly pray that readers may find them instructive and joyful.

Leon C. Le Van
St. Petersburg, Florida

Emanuel Swedenborg

Emanuel Swedenborg was born in Stockholm, Sweden on Jan. 29, 1688. His father was chaplain of the court of Sweden and Bishop of Skara. At Uppsala University, Swedenborg received his Doctor of Philosophy at the age of twenty-one. His main interests were mathematics and engineering. After graduation he traveled extensively throughout Europe visiting the leaders of thought in many fields including mining and astronomy.

In 1718 he was appointed to Sweden's Department of Mines. He was a member of Sweden's House of Nobles. He gave Sweden its first publication of algebra. He led an amazingly productive life writing on many subjects. He has been called the "Aristotle of the North" and the "last universal scholar."

At the age of fifty-six he turned all his great abilities to increasing perception of the Spiritual World. Over the succeeding years he published theological writings which are now translated into many languages throughout the world. This followed his illumination, when his spiritual faculties were opened within. His testification to the real existence of the Lord God the Savior is unmatched in any language. He subscribed himself simply: "Servant of the Lord Jesus Christ."

As the years go by, Swedenborg stands forth increasingly as a world teacher. He tells us internal truths about God and Heaven and the human soul. The faithful seeker of truths is prone to say: "The search is fulfilled. I have found Divine truth. God has shown me the way."

Helen Keller states: "I plunge my hands deep into my large Braille volumes containing Swedenborg's teachings and withdraw them full of the secrets of the Spiritual World." He died in London on March 29, 1772.

To the Reader

Offering these "Poems from Swedenborg" for general reading leaves me with a great sense of unworthiness for so worthy a task. Nonetheless, I must offer them as they are or withdraw them entirely from view. As they come into your hands may they be for you a candle at evening or lamp in the night. Evey truth brings light — in fact is light, light from the Spiritual Sun.

It may be asked, "Can these passages from Swedenborg's writings truly be regarded as valid poems?" It may be they cannot. However, each has a rhythm and even a cadence that lends itself to a free-verse construction, and in that respect they may be called poems. *Arcana* no. 1648 states that angelic speech sometimes flows forth in a sort of "rhythmical cadence." Structured in poetic style, these passages may reach the reader with fresh impact and meaning.

The fairly frequent use of capitalization is another feature that marks these poems. In most cases Swedenborg did not employ capitalization, but good use of capitals instantly identifies subjects of greatest importance. To use them to elevate loftiest subjects such as God, Lord, Universe, Love, Wisdom, Providence, Heaven, etc. above the level of commonplace things may here be permissible.

In putting these poems forth no attempt is made to disguise the fact that Swedenborg is seen as a true revelator from God. The more clearly his writings disclose Creation, Heaven, hell, Divine Love, Divine Wisdom, life, death, Resurrection, the Kingdom of God, and the internal or spiritual sense of the Word, the more value they can yield to new and previous readers.

That readers of these poems may find them clear, simple, and instructive is my prayer. Each in itself is like a small gem in a royal crown or like a precious stone in the holy breastplate. If they are less than that, it is because I have failed to present them in the manner they deserve. I commend these poems to your loving attention, and may "flights of angels" raise them from the printed pages into the higher regions of your mind. L.C.L.

Contents

Contents

Contents

Poetic Renderings

These "Poems from Swedenborg" are poetic renderings from Swedenborg's prose writings. They make use of Swedenborg's own words but are set forth in free-verse style and manner. This rendering gives them readability and freshness that even long time readers of Swedenborg may find stimulating. Please read them with the certainty that it is Swedenborg's own words and language that are here set forth in poetic style.

Part One

Part One 3

Spiritual World

That there is a Spiritual World
Inhabited by spirits and angels
Distinct from the natural world
Inhabited by men
Is a fact which
(Because no angel has descended
and declared it
And no man has ascended
And seen it)
Has been hitherto unknown
Even in the Christian world;
Lest therefore
From ignorance
Of the existence
Of such a world
And the doubts
Respecting the reality
Of Heaven and hell
Which result from such ignorance
Men should be infatuated
To such a degree
As to become
Naturalists and atheists,
It has pleased the Lord
To open my spiritual sight
And (as to my spirit)
To elevate me into Heaven
And to let me down into hell
And to exhibit to my view
The nature of both.
It has thus been made
Evident to me
That there are two worlds
Completely distinct
From each other
As also
That spirits and angels
Live in their own world
And men in theirs
And further that every man
Passes by death
From this world into the other
In which he lives
To Eternity.

SB.3

In the Lord

Those who love
The Lord's Kingdom
Love the Lord above all things
And are consequently
In love to God
More than others
Because the church in Heaven
And on earth
Is the body of the Lord;
For those who are in it
Are in the Lord
And the Lord in them.

T.416

Obtains Life

Man obtains life
By going to the Lord
Because the Lord
Is life itself,
Not only the life of faith
But also
The life of charity.

T.358

Regard

Moral life may be lived
Either out of regard
To the Divine
Or out of regard
To the men in the world;
And a moral life
That is lived out of regard
To the Divine
Is a spiritual life;
In outward form
The two appear alike
But in inward form
They are wholly different.
The one saves man,
The other does not.

H.319

Not Born Spiritual

Man is not
Born of his parents
Into a spiritual life
But only into natural life.
The spiritual life of man
Consists in loving God
Above all things
And in loving the neighbor
As himself,
And this
According to the precepts
Which the Lord has taught
In the Word.

HD.174

The Lord Alone Combats

The Lord alone combats
For man in temptation;
And unless he believes
That the Lord alone
Combats and conquers for him
He undergoes only
An external temptation,
Which is in no respect
Conducive to his salvation.

HD. 195

Falls into Swoon

The great power
That angels have
By means of truths from good
Is shown from this —
That when an evil spirit
Is merely looked at
By the angels
He falls into a swoon
And does not appear
Like a man,
And this until the angel
Turns away his eyes.

H.232

Spiritual Light

The light of Heaven
Is not a natural light
Like the light
Of the world,
But a spiritual light
Because it is from the Lord
As a Sun.
And that Sun
Is the Divine Love.

H.127

Divine Merit

Since all good and truth
Are from the Lord
And nothing from man;
And since good
That comes from man
Is not good in reality,
It plainly follows
That no merit belongs to man
But that all merit
Is due to the Lord alone.

HD.155

Never Turns Away

Those who think
From an enlightened mind
Clearly perceive
When they read the Word
That God never
Turns Himself away from man;
And as He never
Turns Himself away from him
He deals with him
From goodness
Love, and mercy —
That is,
Wills good to him,
Loves him,
And is merciful to him.

H.545

Likes Attract

Every evil in man
Is in conjunction
With those in hell
Who are in like evil
And on the other hand
Every good in man
Is in conjunction
With those in Heaven
Who are in like good.

T.613

Mirror of God

Every one can see
That a man's
Knowledge of God
Is his mirror of God
And that those
Who know nothing of God
Do not see God
In a mirror with its face
Toward them
But in a mirror
With its back toward them
Which does not
Reflect the image
But extinguishes it.

T.11

Life Becomes Death

A man's life
Is from love to the Lord
And faith in Him,
And if this essential element
Of faith and love
That the Lord is God-Man
And Man-God
Is taken away,
Man's life becomes death;
Thus in this way
Man is killed.

T.380

Fully Drawn

The doctrine of genuine truth
May be fully drawn
From the sense
Of the letter of the Word
Since the Word in that sense
Is like a man clothed
With his face bare;
And all things pertaining
To man's faith and life
And thus his Salvation
Are there naked
While the rest are clothed.

T.229

Because He Lives

No one is saved
For the reason
That the Lord
Is known to him,
But because he lives
In accordance with the
Lord's commandments.

P.330

Reception of God

Divine order requires
That man should
Prepare himself
For the reception of God
And in proportion
As he prepares himself
God enters into him
As into his dwelling place
And home.
This preparation is effected
By means of knowledges
Respecting God
And the spiritual things
Pertaining to the church.

T.89

Treasures of Wisdom

Some things shall be stated
That have been
Hitherto unknown
In the learned world,
As much so
As things buried in the earth,
And yet they are
Treasures of wisdom,
And unless they are dug up
And given to the public
Man will toil in vain
To arrive
At any correct knowledge
Of God, faith, charity
And the state
Of his own life.

                                T.362

Light and Glory

The light and glory
Of faith
May be compared
To the beauty of the rainbow
Or of a field of flowers
Or of a blooming garden
In early spring.

                                T.353

Wholly Like Men

It has not been known
Heretofore
That the Word
Exists in the Heavens
Nor could be made known
So long as it was
Unknown in the church
That angels and spirits
Are men in face and body
Wholly like men
In our world.

                                T.240

Removal

The removal of sins
(Which is called
The forgiveness of them)
May be likened
To the casting forth
Of the filth from the camps
Of the children of Israel
Into the desert roundabout
For their camps
Represented Heaven
And the desert hell.

                                T.614

By the Human

Redemption consists in
Subjugating the hells
Restoring the Heavens
To order,
And after this
Re-establishing the church,
After this Redemption
God with His omnipotence
Could only effect
By means of His Human.

                                T.84

Principles

Truth and good
Are the principles
Of all things
In both worlds
The spiritual and the natural;
Also they are the means
By which the Universe
Was created
And through which
The Universe is preserved
And the means as well
By which man
Was created.

                                T.224

Being Filled

The natural man
In whom the spiritual degree
Is opened
Knows that his spiritual mind
Is being filled by the Lord
With thousands of arcana
Of wisdom
And with thousands of delights
Of love
And that he is to come
Into these after death
When he becomes an angel.

DLW.252

Led and Taught

That man is led and taught
By the Lord alone
Means that he lives
From the Lord alone;
For what is led
Is his life's will,
And what is taught
In his life's
Understanding.

P.156

Is Actually There

He who wills and loves
Evil in the world
Wills and loves
The same evil
In the Other life
But he no longer
Suffers himself
To be withdrawn from it.
If therefore
A man is in evil
He is tied to hell
And in respect to his spirit
Is actually there.

H.547

Love Can Choose

It is man's love
That becomes spiritual
And is regenerated;
And it cannot
Become spiritual
Or be regenerated
Unless it knows
(By means of its understanding)
What evil is
And what good is,
And therefore what truth is
And what falsity is.
When it knows this
It can choose
Either one or the other.

DLW.425

Another Sun

That there is any other Sun
Than that of the natural world
Has hitherto been unknown.
The reason is
That the spiritual of man
Has so far passed over
Into his natural
That he does not know
That there is a Spiritual World,
The abode of spirits and angels.

DLW.85

Imbibes Truths

Love imbibes truths
By means
Of its understanding
And not from itself;
For love
Cannot elevate itself
Unless it knows truths.

DLW.422

Many Things

There is a Word
In the Heavens
And it is read
By the angels there
And also by the spirits
Who are below the Heavens;
But that this might not remain
For ever unknown
It has been granted me
To associate
With angels and spirits,
To see the things about them
And afterwards relate
Many things
That I saw and heard.

T.240

God Elevates

No one can think
Above sensual things
And see the truths
Of the church
Unless he acknowledges God
And lives according
To His Commandments
For it is God
Who elevates and enlightens.

T.402

Man

Man is man
So far as he speaks
From sound reason
And looks forward
To his abode in Heaven;
While so far as he speaks
From perverted reason
And looks only
To his abode in the world
So far he is not man.

T.417

In Him

Good has it origin
In the Lord
And likewise truth,
For the Lord is good itself
And truth itself
And in Him
The two are one.

P.10

The Heavenly Marriage

The conjunction
Of good and truth
Is called in Heaven
The Heavenly marriage,
For all who are there
Are in that marriage.
For this reason (in the Word)
Heaven is likened to a marriage
And the Lord is called
The Bridegroom and Husband,
And Heaven
(And the church also)
The Bride and Wife.

T.398

Evils

The evils of those
Who are in the love of rule
From love of self
Are in general as follows:
Contempt of others,
And enmity against those
Who do not favor them.
Hatred, hostility,
Revenge, unmercifulness,
Ferocity and cruelty;
And where such evils prevail
There is also
Contempt of God
And of Divine things.

T.405

Israel's Great Error

The Israelitish nation
Did not acknowledge the Lord
Although the whole
Sacred Scripture
Prophesied of Him
And foretold His Coming.
They rejected Him
Solely for the reason
That he taught them
Of a Heavenly
Instead of an earthly
Kingdom
For they wanted a Messiah
Who would exhalt them
Above all nations
In the whole world
And not a Messiah
Who would have regard
To their Eternal Salvation.

T.205

Many Occupations

There are in Heaven
More functions, services,
And occupations
That can be enumerated,
While in the world
There are few
In comparison.

H.393

Beautiful

It is a matter of importance
To know that everyone's
Human form after death
Is the more beautiful
In proportion
As he has interiorly
Loved Divine truths
And lived according to them.

H.459

Everything Spiritual

The New Jerusalem
Means a New Church
That is to be established
By the Lord.
And since Jerusalem
Signifies the church
It follows that everything
Said of it as a city,
Of its gates, its wall,
The foundations of its wall,
And also its dimensions
Contains a spiritual sense.
For whatever relates
To the church
Is spiritual.

T.197

Mother Earth

In trees
And in all other subjects
Of the vegetable kingdom
There are not two sexes
A masculine and a feminine
But everything there
Is masculine.
The earth alone
Or the soil
Is the common mother
And thus as it were
Feminine
For it receives the seeds
Of all fruits,
Opens them,
Carries them as it were
In a womb
And then nourishes them
And brings them forth —
That is,
Ushers them into the light
Of day
And afterwards clothes
And sustains them.

T.585

What Is Asked?

In the Spiritual World
Into which every man
Comes after death
It is not asked
What your belief has been
Or what your Doctrine
Has been
But what your life has been,
For it is known
That everyone's life
Is such as his belief
And even his Doctrine.

P.101

From God

It is evident to angels
That the created Universe
Is an image
Representative of God-Man
And that it is
His Love and Wisdom
Which are presented
In an image
In the Universe.

DLW.52

Still Do Them

If men abstain
From doing evils
Not because
They are sins against God
But because they fear the laws
Or the loss of reputation
They still do them
In their spirit;
For what a man thinks
In his spirit in this world
That he does
After he leaves this world
When he becomes a spirit.

P.101

God Rendered

God first rendered
His Infinity finite
By means of substances
Emitted from Himself
From which His
Nearest surrounding sphere,
Which constitutes
The Sun of the Spiritual World,
Came into existence:
And then
Through that Sun
He perfected
The other surrounding spheres
Even to the outmost,
Which consists
Of passive materials,
And in this manner
By means of degrees
He rendered the world
More and more finite.

T.33

No End

The Infinity of God
Has been made evident to me
Both from the angelic Heaven
And from hell
In that these
Are ordered and arranged
In innumerable Societies
Or congregated bodies
In accordance
With all the varieties
Of the love of good or evil,
Each individual
Being allotted a place
In accordance with his love;
For there the whole Human Race
From the creation of the world
Is gathered together,
And to ages of ages
Will be gathered.

T.32

Eternal Endeavor

As fructifications
And multiplications
Have not failed
From the beginning
Of Creation
Nor will ever fail
To Eternity,
It follows
That in that ability
There is an endeavor
To an Eternal
Self-propagation.

P.56

From Infinity

The Creation of the Universe
And of all things of it
Cannot be said
To have been wrought
From Space to Space,
Or from Time to Time,
Thus progressively
And successively
But from Eternity
And from Infinity.

DLW.156

Fleeting Shadow

Any one may come
Into spiritual freedom
If he is willing to think
That life is Eternal
And that the temporary
Enjoyment and bliss
Of life in Time
Is but a fleeting shadow
Compared
With the never-ending
Enjoyment and bliss
Of life in Eternity.

P.73

Born Again

No one can come
Into the Kingdom of God
Unless he has been
Born again,
For the reason
That man by inheritance
Is born into evils
Of every kind
But with an ability
To become spiritual
By the removal of those evils,
And unless he becomes
Spiritual
He cannot come into Heaven.

P.83

Holy Scripture

The entire Holy Scripture
Teaches that there is a God,
Because in its inmosts
It is nothing but God
That is —
It is nothing but the Divine
That goes forth from God;
For it was
Dictated by God;
And from God
Nothing can go forth
Except what is God
And is called Divine.
This the Holy Scripture is
In its inmosts.

T.6

Inmost Angels

The angels
In the Inmost Heaven
Are the most beautiful
For they are forms
Of celestial love.

H.459

Must Acknowledge

The means of Salvation
Relate to these two points:
That evils must be shunned
Because they are contrary
To the Divine laws
In the Decalogue
And there must be
An acknowledgment
That there is a God.
This everyone can do
Provided he does not
Love evils.

P.329

In Every Religion

The Lord provides
That there shall be
Everywhere a Religion
And that in every Religion
There shall be
The two essentials
Of Religion
Which are
To acknowledge God
And refrain from evils
Because they are
Sins against God.

P.328

Same Looks

If the thought and will
Are good
The deeds and works
Are good
But if the thought and will
Are evil
The deeds and works
Are evil
Although in outward looks
They are the same.

H.472

From the Saved

Because Divine Providence
Has as its end
A Heaven
From the Human Race
It follows
That the reformation
And regeneration of man
(Thus his Salvation)
Is what Divine Providence
Especially looks to;
For from those
That have been
Saved or regenerated
Heaven exists.

P.58

Appears Present

In the Spiritual World
When anyone there
Thinks about another
And wishes to speak with him
The other immediately
Appears present.
This is a common occurrence
And never fails.

P.326

No Death

Because man was created
To be spiritual
As well as natural
God has provided the Word
In which He has revealed
Not only Himself
But also that there is
A Heaven and a hell
And that in one or other
Of these
Every man is to live
To Eternity.

T.22

Steps to Wisdom

I have sometimes
Talked with angels
About wisdom
And they said
They represent wisdom
To themselves
As a palace
Magnificent
And highly adorned
The ascent to which
Is by twelve steps
And that only from the Lord
Can anyone reach
Even the first step.

P.36

Towards Eternal Spring

Those in Heaven
Are continually advancing
Towards the spring of life
With a greater advance
Towards a more joyful
And happy spring
The more thousands of years
They live
And this to Eternity.

H.414

Inner World

Every one after death
Is first introduced
Into the world
Which is called
The World of Spirits
And which is intermediate
Between Heaven and hell;
And in that world
He is prepared
For Heaven if he is good
And for hell if he is evil.

CL.48

Wise and Simple

All received into Heaven
Who have loved truth and good
For the sake of truth and good;
Therefore those
That have loved much
Are called the wise
And those that have
Loved little
Are called the simple.

H.350

In the Lord

Since the Lord
Is very Man
And Heaven is His image,
To be in Heaven
Is called
Being in the Lord.

P.65

Three Heavens

There are three Heavens
A Highest
A Middle,
And a Lowest;
And those who by regeneration
Acquire love to the Lord
Enter the Highest Heaven;
Those who acquire
Love to the neighbor
Enter the Middle Heaven;
And those who merely practice
External charity
But at the same time
Acknowledge the Lord
As God,
The Redeemer and Savior
Enter the Lowest Heaven.
All these are saved
But in different ways.

T.580

Never Cease to Wonder

In the Christian world
It is wholly unknown
That Heaven and hell
Are from the Human Race
For it is believed
That in the beginning
Angels were created
And Heaven was thus formed;
Also that the Devil or Satan
Was an angel of light
But having rebelled
He was cast down with his crew
And thus hell was formed.
The angels
Never cease to wonder
At such a belief
In the Christian world,
And still more
That nothing is really known
About Heaven
When that is in fact
The primary principle
Of all doctrine
In the church.

H.311

Shining Love

All observation
In Heaven attests
That the Divine
That goes forth from the Lord
And that affects angels
And makes Heaven
Is love;
For all who are in Heaven
Are forms of love and charity
And appear
In ineffable beauty
With love shining forth
From their faces
And from every particular
Of their life.

H.17

Can Be Raised

The human mind is divided
Into three regions;
From the highest region
Man looks to God;
From the middle region
To the world;
And from the lowest
To himself.
The mind being such
It can be raised up
And can raise itself
To God and Heaven.

T.395

Immeasurable

One can see
How great the delight
Of Heaven must be
From the fact
That it is the delight
Of every one in Heaven
To share
His delights and blessings
With others;
And as such is the character
Of all that are in the Heavens
It is clear how immeasurable
Is the delight of Heaven.

H.399

Flame Dies

Those who have genuine charity
Have zeal for what is good.
And that zeal may appear
In the external man
Like anger and flaming fire
But its flame dies out
And is quieted
As soon as his adversary
Returns to reason.

T.408

When Love Descends

As natural love
Can ascend by degrees
And become
Spiritual and celestial,
In the same way
It can descend by degrees
And become
Sensual and corporeal;
And it does descend
So far as it loves dominion
From no love of use,
But solely
From love of self.

DLW.424

Jehovah the Lord

Jehovah is called
The Lord from Eternity,
Since Jehovah
Assumed a Human
That He might save men
From hell,
He then commanded
His disciples to call Him Lord.
Therefore in the New Testament
Jehovah is called "the Lord."

DLW.282

Chastity Enters

So far as any one
Removes evil,
So far a capacity is given
For good to succeed
In its place;
And further,
So far as evil is hatred,
So far good is loved.
Consequently,
So far as whoredom is renounced,
So far
The chastity of marriage enters.

CL.147

Became the Word

He who thinks and speaks
Nothing but the truth
Becomes that truth,
And he who wills and does
Only what is good
Becomes that good;
And as the Lord fulfilled
All the Divine truth
All the Divine good
Contained in the Word,
He became good itself
And truth itself
That is, the Word.

T.263

All Would Be Saved

If men could be saved
By mercy apart from means
All would be saved,
Even those in hell,
Because the Lord
Is mercy itself,
Love itself,
And goodness itself.
The Lord desires
The salvation of all,
And the damnation of none.

H.524

Mutual Desire

The states of conjugial love
Are innocence, peace,
Tranquility
Inmost friendship,
Full confidence,
And a mutual desire
Of mind and heart
To do each other
Every good.

CL.156

In the Garden

The unregenerate man
Is like one
Who is in the Garden of Eden
And who eats
Of the tree of the knowledge
Of good and evil
And is therefore banished
From the Garden;
But the regenerate man
Is like one
Who is in the Garden
And eats of the Tree of Life.

T.606

Heaven in Man

Love of self
And love of the world
Reign in hell
And also constitute
Hell in man;
But love to the Lord
And love towards the neighbor
Are Heavenly loves
And these reign in Heaven
And also constitute
Heaven in man.

T.400

Microcosm

The higher
Or spiritual region
Of the human mind
Is a heaven in miniature
While the lower
Or natural region
Is a world in miniature
And for this reason
Man was called by the ancients
A microcosm,
A little world.

T.604

God Most Present

In spiritual temptations
Man is apparently left
To himself alone
Although he is not,
For God is then
Most nearly present
In man's inmosts
And sustains him.
Therefore when man conquers
In temptations
He is inmostly conjoined
With God.

T.126

In the Word

It is idle to believe
That the Lord will appear
In the clouds of heaven
In Person;
But He is to appear
In the Word
Which is from Him
And therefore is Himself.

T.777

For Their Sake

The Lord
Did not create the Universe
For His own sake
But for the sake of those
With whom He is to be
In Heaven
Since Divine Love is such
That it wishes to give
Its own to another,
And so far
As it can do this
It is in its being,
In its peace,
And in its blessedness.

P.27

Not Changed by Death

I can testify
From much experience
That it is impossible
To implant the life of Heaven
In those who in the world
Lived a life opposite
To the life of Heaven.
There were some who believed
That when after death
They should hear
Divine truths from the angels
They would readily
Accept them and believe them
And live a different life
And thus be received
Into Heaven,
But the experiment was made
With great numbers
And it was permitted
To teach them
That repentance was not
Possible after death.
Some understood truths
And seemed to accept them.
Others were unwilling
To hear them and at once
Rejected them.
Others wished to have the life
They had contracted
In the world
Taken away from them
And to have angelic life
Infused in its place.
This too was permitted
But as soon as their own life
Was taken away
They fell as if dead
With their mental powers
Gone.
The angels declare
It would be easier
To change a horned owl
Into a bird of Paradise
Than to change an infernal spirit
Into an angel of Heaven.

H.527

Spiritual Freedom

The life of man's spirit
Consists in his
Freedom of choice
In spiritual things.
The angels weep
When they hear it but said
That freedom of choice
Is denied
By many ministers
Of the church
At this day,
And they call this denial
Madness upon madness.

T.482

Angel of Jehovah

Sometimes the Lord
So fills an angel
With His Divine
That the angel does not know
That he is not the Lord.
Thus were the angels filled
That were seen
By Abraham, Hagar,
And Gideon
And therefore
They called themselves
Jehovah.

P.96

Images and Likeness

Man's being an
"Image of God"
Means that he is
A recipient
Of the Divine Wisdom
And his being
A "likeness of God"
Means that he is a recipient
Of the Divine Love.

P.328

Hundred Thousand

Lest those who think
From worldly wisdom
Should any longer
Confound and mislead
The simple in faith and heart,
And induce infernal darkness
Respecting God and Heaven
And eternal life,
The interiors of my spirit
Have been opened by the Lord
And I have thus been permitted
To talk with all
After their decease
With whom I was ever acquainted
In the life of the body —
With some for days,
With some for months,
And with some for a year;
And also with so many others
That I should not
Exaggerate
If I should say
A hundred thousand.

H.312

Origin of Worlds

They who deduce
The origin of worlds
From any other source
Than the Divine Love
Operating by Divine Wisdom
Fall into hallucinations
Like those of persons
Disordered in the brain
Who see spectres as men,
Phantoms as luminous objects,
And imaginary entities
As real figures;
For the created Universe
Is a coherent work
Originating from Love
Operating by Wisdom.

SB.5

Breath of Life

The soul
Is not life in itself
But is a recipient
Of life from God
Who is Life in itself;
And all influx belongs to life,
Thus is from God.
This is meant by the words:
"Jehovah God breathed
Into the nostrils of the man
The breath of life
And man became
A living soul."

SB.8

Conjoined Within

Good flows into man
By an internal way
Or that of the soul
But truths
By an external way
Or that of hearing and sight
And they are conjoined
In man's interiors
By the Lord.

HD.23

In Every Age

From the light of nature
Nothing can be known
Concerning the Lord,
Concerning Heaven and hell,
Concerning the life of man
After death,
Nor concerning Divine Truths
By which man acquires
Spiritual and eternal life.
Therefore
In every age of the world
There has been a Revelation.

W.H.6

New Joy

Most of those
Who had recently died
When they saw themselves
To be living men as before
And in a like state
Were moved by new joy
At being alive
Saying that they
Had not believed
That it would be so.
They greatly wondered
That they should have lived
In such
Ignorance and blindness
About the state of their life
After death.

H.312

Direct Opposites

Loves of self
And of the world
Tend to destroy
The joys of Heaven
And are thus
Direct opposites
Of Heavenly loves,
Which desire to share.

H.399

First and Chief

Heaven within man
Is acknowledging the Divine
And being led
By the Divine.
The first and chief thing
Of every Religion
Is to acknowledge the Divine;
A Religion that does not
Acknowledge the Divine
Is no Religion.

H.319

Well Known

That the Lord was conceived
By Jehovah the Father
And thus is God
By virtue of such conception
Is a truth well known
In the church:
Also that He rose again
With His whole body.

HD.286

Are Not Truths

Truths without good
Are not truths
Because they have
No life;
For all the life of truths
Is from good;
They are as a body
Without a soul.

HD.22

Nothing Comparable

The angels said
That although the style
Of the Word seems simple
In the sense of a letter
It is such
That nothing can be compared to it
In excellence
Since Divine wisdom lies concealed
Not only in the meaning
As a whole
But also in each word;
And in Heaven
The wisdom shines forth.
They wished to declare
That this wisdom
Is the very light of Heaven
Because it is
Divine truth.

H.310

Conjunction Granted

Truths teach
How man ought to live;
And when man
Is moved by truths
For the sake of truths,
Which is done
When he loves to live
According to them,
He is led by the Lord;
And conjunction with Heaven
Is granted him;
And he becomes spiritual,
And after death
An angel of Heaven.

E.820

To Be Seen

All truth
Wishes to be seen
Because it belongs
To the light of Heaven;
And truth that is not seen
May be falsified
In many ways.
And falsified truth
Is falsity.

E.781

"First Fruits"

"First fruits to God
And to the Lamb"
Mean those who will be
Of the New Church
Which is called
The New Jerusalem,
Who acknowledge
The Lord's Divine Human
And live a life of love
According to the Lord's
Commandments in the Word.

E.865

Noble Man

As man is formed,
So he is perfected
In intelligence and wisdom
And becomes a man;
For no man is a man
From his natural mind;
For from that
He is rather a beast
But he becomes a man
Through intelligence
And wisdom from the Lord,
And so far
As he is intelligent and wise
He is a noble man
And an angel of Heaven.

E.790

Is in Pride

Every one
Who is in the love of self
When he writes or preaches
Is in pride;
And pride derives all things
From man's own proprium;
Consequently it is called
The pride
Of self-intelligence.

E.825

Higher Place

To shun evils and do goods
For the sake of reputation
And one's own honor
Is not hurtful
Provided the Word and Religion
Hold the higher place
And constitute the head,
And self and the world
Hold the lower place
And constitute the feet.

E.825

Proper Duties

In the duties
Proper to husbands
The primary agent
Is understanding,
Thought, and wisdom;
Whereas
In the duties
Proper to wives
The primary agent
Is will,
Affection, and love;
And the wife from the latter
Performs her duties,
And the husband
From the former
Performs his.

CL.175

Universals

The reason why good and truth
Are the universals of Creation
Is because these two
Are in the Lord God,
The Creator;
Yea, they are Himself;
For He is essential Divine good
And essential Divine truth.

CL.84

Becomes Evil

If man becomes natural only,
He loves only
Corporeal and worldly things;
And so far as he loves these,
So far as he does not love
Celestial and spiritual
Things
And does not look to God.
And so far
He becomes evil.

DLW.345

Primary Principle

There are two things
Which constitute
The life of Heaven in man —
The good of love
And the truth of faith.
Man derives his life
From God
And in no respect or degree
From himself;
Therefore,
The primary principle
Of the church
Is to acknowledge God,
To believe in Him,
And to love Him.

HD.281

Essential Chastity

Love truly conjugial
Is essential chastity;
And the love
Opposite to it,
Which is called adulterous,
Is essential unchastity;
So far therefore
As anyone is purified
From the latter love
So far he is chaste.

CL.139

Acknowledged

It is acknowledged
In the Christian world
That no mortal
Could have been saved
Unless the Lord
Had come into the world;
And this is why
The Lord is called
"The First and the Last."

P.124

Two Worlds

The Universe in general
Is divided
Into two worlds,
The spiritual and the natural.
In the Spiritual World
Are angels and spirits;
In the natural world, men.
In external appearance
These two worlds
Are entirely alike,
So alike
That they cannot
Be distinguished
But as to
Internal appearance
They are entirely unlike.

DLW.163

Becomes Spiritual

Everyone
In the Christian world
Since the Lord's Coming
Has the ability to become
Spiritual
As he becomes spiritual
Solely from the Lord
Through the Word.

T.501

When Holiness Remains

The sense
Of the letter of the Word
May be turned
In any direction.
If it is turned to what is false
Its external holiness
Perishes and with it
Its external holiness;
But if turned to what is true
Its holiness remains.

T.207

Palaces in Heaven

I have seen palaces in Heaven
Of such magnificence
As cannot be described.
They glittered above
As if made of pure gold
And below as if made
Of precious stones
Some more splendid than others.
Words and knowledge
Are inadequate to describe
The decorations
That adorned the rooms.

H.185

All Except Body

When man passes
From the natural world
Into the Spiritual
As he does when he dies
He carries with him
All his possessions —
That is, everything
That belongs to him
As a man
Except his earthly body.

H.461

Born of God

Who denies
Or is able to deny
That every good of love
And every truth of wisdom
Is solely from God
And that so far
As man receives these
From God
He lives from God
And is said to be
Born of God
Or born again.

T.471

Fiery Zeal

Zeal prevails with enthusiasts
And also with those
Who are in the utmost
Falsities of doctrine
And even with those
Who despise the Word.
For zeal in itself considered
Is a fire of the natural man
But if it has within it
A love of truth
It is like the sacred fire
That descended on the Apostles.

T.146

Divine Victories

All the strength,
Energy,
And power of God
Belong to Divine Truth
From the Divine Good.
This explains
Why Jehovah God
Came down as Divine Truth
Which is the Word.

T.86

Love the Lord

Enlightenment is given
To those who love truths
And who make them
Uses of life
Because such are
In the Lord
And the Lord is in them,
For the Lord
Is Truth itself
And men love the Lord
When they live
In accordance
With His Divine truths.

T.231

Divine Human

It is believed that the Lord
As to His Human
Not only was but still is
The son of Mary.
It is true that He was
The son of Mary
But not true
That He still is;
For by the acts of redemption
He put off the human
From the mother
And put on a Human
From the Father,
And this is why
The Human of the Lord
Is Divine
And in Him
God is Man and Man is God.

T.102

Down Through Heaven

Inasmuch
As the Divine Truth
Passed down
Through the Heavens
Even to the world
It became adapted
To angels in Heaven
And also to men
In the world.

T.85

Partners of Angels

When men's evils
Have been put away
Such appear in Heaven
Before the angels
As beautiful human beings
And as partners
Of the angels.

P.121

As if from Infancy

Everyone after death
Comes into the Society
Of his own —
That is, of those
Who are in a like love,
He recognizes these
As relatives
And as friends,
And what is then wonderful
When he meets them
And sees them
It is as if he had been
Acquainted with them
From infancy.

P.338

With Angels

Conjugial love is called
Celestial and spiritual
Because it is with
The angels of Heaven;
Celestial as with the angels
Of the highest Heaven
(These being called
Celestial angels)
And spiritual
As with the angels
Beneath that Heaven,
These being called
Spiritual angels.

CL.64

Rarely Manifest

The more nearly
Anyone is conjoined
With the Lord
The happier he becomes,
But this happiness
Is rarely manifest
In the world.

P.41

Collected

All the beatitudes,
Satisfactions,
Delights,
Pleasantnesses,
And pleasures
Which the Lord the Creator
Could possibly confer
Upon man
Are collected
Into conjugial love.

CL.68

Above Every Love

None can be principled
In love truly conjugial
But those who receive it
From the Lord,
Because this love
Considered in its origin
Is celestial,
Spiritual, holy,
Pure, clean,
Above every love implanted
In the angels of Heaven
And the men of the church.

CL.71

Universe

This vast system
Which is called the Universe
Is a work coherent as a unit
From things first
To things last
Because in creating it
God had a single end in view
Which was an Angelic Heaven
From the Human Race;
And all things
Of which the world consists
Are means to that end.

T.13

Idle Words

Many in the world
Attribute all things
To themselves
And their own prudence
Or what they can not
Attribute to themselves
They call accidental or casual
Not knowing
That human prudence
Is nothing
And that
Accidental and casual
Are idle words.

P.70

Cannot Deny

To each evil spirit
All his evils, villainies,
Robberies, artifices
And deceits are made clear
And are brought forth
From his very memory,
And his guilt
Is fully established,
Nor is there
Any possible room for denial
Because all the circumstances
Are exhibited together.

H.462

Good Will

Those who are
In the love of self
And the world
Have no good will
For any but themselves,
While those who are
In love to the Lord
And love towards the neighbor
Have good will towards all.

P.106

Heaven First

It is in accordance
With Divine order
That a new Heaven
Should be formed
Before a new church
Is established on earth,
For the church
Is both internal and external
And the internal church
Makes one
With the church in Heaven
Thus with Heaven itself,
And what is internal
Must be formed
Before its external.
Just so far
As this new Heaven
Which constitutes
The internal of the church
Increases
Does the New Jerusalem —
That is,
The New Church,
Descend from it.

T.784

Like a Star

When wisdom
Is conjoined with love
It is like
The abiding light of the sun
And like a fixed star.

P.35

Not Put Asunder

Man's not putting asunder
What God has joined together
Means that good
Is not to be separated
From truth.

H.372

In Fullness

In the sense of the letter
The Word is
In its fullness,
Its holiness,
And its power,
Because the two prior senses
Which are called
Spiritual and celestial
Exist simultaneously
In the natural sense,
Which is the sense
Of the letter.

T.214

Descending Influx

It is well known
That all the good of love
And all the truth of faith
Flow into man from God
And that no portion of them
Is from man himself;
And whatever flows from God
Flows into his soul
And by the soul
Into the rational mind
And by this into the organs
Which consitute the body.

SB.8

Wise Man

The wise man
Thinks above sensual things
And when thought is elevated
Above what is sensual
It enters into clearer light
And finally
Into the light of Heaven;
From this
Man has perception of truth
Which is properly intelligence.

T.402

Chiefly of Infants

The New Heaven is composed
Both of Christians and Gentiles
But chiefly of infants
From all parts of the world
Who have died
Since the Lord's Coming;
For all these were received
By the Lord
And educated in Heaven.

HD.3

Impossible

It is impossible to believe
That Heaven and hell
Are from the human race
If it is believed
That no man can go there
Until the end
Of the world.

H.312

Extinguish

"Thou hast a name
That thou livest
And art dead."
They are called "dead"
Who believe
Life to be from nature
And thus believe
Nature to be the light of life
And thereby bury,
Suffocate, and extinguish
Every idea of God,
Of Heaven,
And of Eternal life.
In consequence of so doing
Such persons
Are like owls
Which see light in darkness
And darkness in light.

SB.10

Form One Heaven

The new Heaven is distinct
From the Ancient Heavens
Which were formed
Before the Coming of the Lord.
At the same time
There is
Such an orderly connection
Established between them
That together they form
But one Heaven.

HD.4

No Pity

The Jewish nation
(Because it had the Word)
Was likened by the Lord
To a rich man who was clothed
In purple and fine linen
And fared sumptuously
Every day
And yet did not gain
Enough truth and good
From the Word
To have pity upon poor Lazarus
Who lay at his door
Full of sores.

T.246

Still Continue

I have talked with some
In the Spiritual World
Who lived many centuries ago
And who had
Confirmed themselves
In the falsities
Of their Religion
And I found
That they still continued
Steadfastly in them.

T.255

Appearances

God is love itself,
Mercy itself,
And Good itself,
And such a Being
Cannot be angry,
Wrathful, or vengeful.
Those things
Are attributed to God
In the Word
Because such is the appearance.
These are appearances
Of truth.

T.256

Profane Mixture

Great care
Is taken by the Lord
Lest truth be conjoined
To evil,
And the false of evil
To good.
Profanation arises
From such a mixture.

HD.21

Not Condemned

In many places in the Word
Anger, wrath, and vengeance
Are attributed to God
And He is said
To punish,
To cast into hell,
To tempt,
And other like things.
He who believes this
In simplicity like a child
And in consequence fears God
And avoids sinning against Him
Is not condemned
For that simple belief.

T.256

Must Pray

The first thing of reformation
Is to refrain from sins,
To shun them,
And turn away from them;
But that he may
Refrain from them,
Shun them,
And turn away from them,
A man must
Pray to the Lord for help.

E.837

Rarely Punished

Every man can freely
Think as he wishes,
As well against God
As for God;
And he that thinks against God
Is rarely punished
In the natural world,
Because there
He is always in a state
To be reformed;
But he is punished
After death.

P.249

Miracles

All miracles
Wrought by the Lord,
And all miracles
Described in the Word
Included in them
The holy things
Of Heaven and the church;
And for this reason
Those miracles were Divine,
And were thus distinguished
From miracles
Not Divine.

E.899

Easily Rejects Falsities

When those who are
In a spiritual affection
For truth
Imbibe falsities of any kind
They easily reject them
When they hear truths
Either in this world
Or in the other.
For this reason
Those who are in this affection
Are perfected
In intelligence and wisdom
To Eternity.

F.867

Receives the Lord

That which goes forth
From the Lord as a Sun
Is Divine truth;
And that which goes forth
From the Lord
Is the Lord;
Consequently,
He that receives truth
From a spiritual love
Because it is truth
Receives the Lord.

E.863

Lives His Religion

Good works are all things
That a man does, writes,
Preaches, and speaks
Not from self but from the Lord;
And he acts, writes
Preaches, and speaks
From the Lord
When he is living
According to the laws
Of his Religion.

E.825

Lord Alone Is Man

Because the angels
Have no perception
Of an invisible Divine
(Which they call
A Divine devoid of form)
But perceive rather
A visible Divine
In human form,
They are accustomed to say
That the Lord alone is man
And that it is from Him
That they are men,
And that every one is a man
In the measure
Of his reception
Of the Lord.
By receiving the Lord
They mean receiving
Good and truth,
Since the Lord
Is in His good
And in His truth.
This they call
Wisdom and intelligence.

H.80

Intentions

The wise
Do not think about works
But about the life
That is in the works —
Namely,
About the intention.
This is especially true
Of the angels
Who are with man;
They do not see his works,
They see only
The intentions of his mind
And conclude therefrom
What the man's state is.

E.185

Written by the Lord

The "book of life"
Means that from the Lord
Which has been written
In man's spirit —
That is,
In his heart and soul
(Or what is the same)
In his love and faith;
And what has been written
By the Lord in man
Is Heaven.

E.199

Two Distinct Loves

In Heaven there are
Two distinct loves —
Love to the Lord
And love towards the neighbor;
In the inmost or third Heaven
Love to the Lord;
In the second or middle Heaven
Love towards the neighbor.
They both go forth
From the Lord,
And they both make Heaven.

H.15

Leads Their Prayers

Worship with those
Who live a moral life
From a spiritual origin
Is truly
A worship of God,
For their prayers
Are raised up into Heaven
And are heard;
For the Lord
Leads their prayers
Through Heaven
To Himself.

E.182

Unseeing Mole

A man who reads the Word
Not under the Lord's auspices
But under the auspices
Of his own intelligence
Thinks himself a lynx
And better sighted than Argus
And yet he inwardly
Sees not a shred of truth
But only what is false,
And under self-persuasion
This falsity seems to him
Like a Polar star
Towards which he directs
All the sails of his thought
And then he no more sees truths
Than a mole.

T.165

Shown by Jehovah

The Tabernacle
Built by Moses
In the wilderness
Represented
Heaven and the church
And therefore the form of it
Was shown by Jehovah
On Mount Sinai.

T.220

No Wish

Those that have no wish
To understand anything
Except what pertains
To the world and its nature
And no wish to understand
What moral and spiritual
Good and truth are
Cannot be raised from knowledge
Into understanding,
Still less into wisdom.

P.75

Through Angelic Heavens

The Word in its bosom
Is spiritual
Because it descended
From Jehovah the Lord
And passed through
The angelic Heavens;
And in its descent
The Divine
(Which in itself is
Ineffable and unperceivable)
Became adapted
To the perception of angels
And finally
To the perception of men.

T.193

Divine Word

Such as Heaven is
Such also is the Lord's Word.
In its outmost sense
It is natural;
In its interior sense
It is spiritual;
And in its inmost sense
Celestial;
And in each of these senses
It is Divine.
Thus it is adapted
To the angels
Of the three Heavens
And also to man.

T.195

Marriage Love

No one can be
In true marriage love
Unless he acknowledges
The Lord and His Divine.
Without that acknowledgment
The Lord cannot flow in.

H.376

Internal Dictate

As a consequence
Of the Divine influx
In the souls of men
There is in every man
An internal dictate
That there is a God
And that He is one.
And yet there are some
Who deny God
And some who acknowledge
More Gods than one
And some who worship
Images as gods
Which is possible
Because such have blocked up
The interiors
Of their reason
Or understanding
With wordly
And corporeal things
Thereby obliterating
Their first or childhood idea
Respecting God.

T.9

Word of Life

Because God is Love itself
And Wisdom itself
He is Life itself.
It is said in John
"The Word was with God
And the Word was God
In Him was life
And the life
Was the light of men.
By "God" the Divine Love
Is meant
And by the "Word"
The Divine Wisdom.

T.39

Faith and Life

Those who know
Nothing about the Lord
(Like most of those
In the two divisions of the Globe
Called Asia and Africa)
If they believe in one God
And live by the precepts
Of the own religion
Are saved by their faith
And life.

T.107

Why God Descended

Jehovah God
Came down into the world
As Divine Truth
In order
That He might work Redemption,
And Redemption consists
In subjugating the Hells,
Restoring the Heavens
To order,
And after this
Establishing a church.

T.86

Neighbor Love

To love the neighbor as oneself
Consists solely
In not acting
Insincerely or unjustly
Towards him,
Not holding him in hatred,
Not burning
With revenge against him,
Not reviling or defaming him,
Not committing adultery
With his wife,
And not doing
Other like things against him.

P.94

Sees Own Way

In the Spiritual World
There are actually ways
That lead
To every Society of Heaven
And to every society of hell;
And there each one
(As if from himself)
Sees his own way,
Because there is a way there
For every love,
And the love reveals the way
And leads one to his fellows.
Other ways
Than the way of his love
No one sees.

P.60

Robbers

The love of self is the same
As that of robbers
Who kiss each other
So long as they are engaged
In robberies
But afterwards
Burn with a desire
To kill each other
In order to take
All the plunder.

T.45

From Human Race

Heaven is not made up
Of angels created such
From the beginning,
And hell did not originate
In any devil
Created an angel of light
And cast down from Heaven
But both Heaven and hell
Are from the Human Race.

P.27

Riches in Heaven

The Heavens
Are divided into Societies;
And those who are eminent
And rich
Are to be found
In every Society.
The eminent there
Are in such glory
And the rich
In such abundance
That the glory and abundance
Of the world
Are almost nothing
In comparison.
But all the eminent there
Are wise
And all the rich
Abound in knowledge.

E.1190

Work of Saving

The Divine Providence
Is unceasingly in the work
Of saving men
But no more can be saved
Than are willing
To be saved

P.333

Complex

Love is the complex
Of all varieties of goodness;
And wisdom the complex
Of all varieties of truth;
But both the latter and former
Are from God
Who is Love itself
And thus good itself
And is Wisdom itself
And thus truth itself.

T.38

Virtues

Spiritual virtues with men
Are the love of Religion,
Charity, truth, conscience,
Innocence, and many more.
These virtues
May in general be referred
To love and zeal for Religion,
For the public good,
For a man's country,
For his fellow citizens,
For his parents,
For his married partner,
And for his children.
In all these
Justice and judgment
Have dominion.

CL.164

Born for Heaven

Man is born for Heaven
Although he does not
Enter Heaven
Unless he becomes
Spiritual
And he can become spiritual
Only by means
Of regeneration.

T.574

Truth Teaches

Truth teaches man
In whom he ought to believe
And what
He ought to believe,
Also, what he ought to do,
Thus how he ought to will;
For whatever one does
He does from the will
In accordance
With his understanding.

T.587

Spiritual Sun

The Sun
Of the Spiritual World
Is nothing but love
From Jehovah God
Who is in the midst of it.
From that Sun
Heat and light go forth.
The heat that goes forth
In its essence is Love
And the light
That goes forth
In its essence is Wisdom.

T.75

Why Impossible

Since it is impossible
For God to damn any one
Who lives well
And believes aright,
So on the other hand
It is impossible
For Him to save any one
Who lives wickedly
And therefore believes
What is false.

T.341

Faith in God

Saving Faith
Is faith in God the Savior
Because He is God and Man
And He is in the Father
And the Father in Him;
Thus they are one;
Therefore those
Who go to him
At the same time
Go to the Father also,
Thus to the one
And only God.

T.337

Fire of Love

It is known that in the Word
(And in the language of preachers)
"Fire" is mentioned
To express Divine Love;
Thus it is usual to pray
That Heavenly fire
May fill the heart
And kindle holy desires
To worship God;
The reason of which is
Because fire corresponds to love
And thence signifies it.
Hence it is
That Jehovah God was seen by Moses
As a fire in a bush;
As also
By the children of Israel
At Mount Sinai;
And that fire was commanded
To be perpetually kept
Upon the altar,
And the lights of the candlesticks
In the Tabernacle
To be lighted every evening.
These commands were given
Because fire signifies
Love.

SB.6

Divine

The human of the Lord
Is Divine
Because it was derived
From the *esse* of the Father
Which was the Lord's soul.

HD.305

For Man's Sake

The Lord does not desire
Glory from man
For the sake of Himself
But for the sake
Of man's salvation.

HD.310

New Earth

Something shall now be said
Concerning the "new earth."
By the "new earth"
Is understood
A new church on earth
For when a former church
Ceases to exist
Then a new one
Is established by the Lord.

HD.5

Not Now Her Son

By means of
Temptations and victories
The Lord expelled
All that was hereditary
From the mother
And put off the human
Which He had from her
Till at length
He was no longer her son.

HD.302

Heavens Distinguished

There are three angelic Heavens,
A supreme
Which is also called
The Third Heaven
Inhabited by angels
Of the supreme degree;
A middle
Which is also called
The Second Heaven
Inhabited by angels
Of the middle degree;
And a lowest
Which is also called
The First Heaven
Inhabited by angels
Of the lowest degree.
Those Heavens are distinguished
According the their degrees
Of love and wisdom.

SB.16

PartTwo

Commanded

In order that the man
Of the New Church
May not wander about
Like the man of the old
In the shade that obscures
The letter of the Word
Especially in respect
To Heaven and hell
And man's life after death
And in respect
To the Lord's Coming.
It has pleased the Lord
To open the sight of my spirit
And thus introduce me
Into the Spiritual World
And permit me
Not only to talk
With spirits and angels,
Relatives and friends,
And even with
Kings and princes
Who have finished their course
In the natural world
But also to see
The wonders of Heaven
And the miseries of hell
And thus to learn
That man after death
Does not abide
In some indefinite place
In the earth
Nor fly about blind and dumb
In the air or in vacancy
But lives as a man
In a substantial body
In a more perfect state
Than before.
I have been
Commanded by the Lord
To make known various things
That I have seen and heard
Respecting Heaven and hell
And respecting
The Last Judgment.

T.771

In One Person

The Lord
By the acts of redemption
United Himself to the Father
And the Father
United Himself to Him
Thus reciprocally and mutually.
From that reciprocal union
It is very evident
That God became Man
And Man became God
In one Person
Like soul and body.

T.101

Inflowings

Every rational man
As soon as he hears it
Acknowledges the truth
That evil cannot flow from good
Or good flow from evil
Because they are opposites.
From good
Nothing but good can flow
And from evil
Nothing but evil.

P.327

In His Spirit

When a man
Believes any evil
To be allowable
He releases it
From internal restraint
And is withheld from doing it
Only by external restraints
Which are fears;
And because his spirit
Then favors that evil
He does it continually
In his spirit.

P.81

Church In Heaven

"Entering into the sheepfold"
Is entering
Into the church
And also into Heaven.
It is entering also
Into Heaven
Because Heaven and the church
Make one,
And nothing makes Heaven
Except the church
That is in it.
Consequently
As the Lord
Is the Bridegroom and Husband
Of the church
So is He also
The Bridegroom and Husband
Of Heaven.

                              T.380

Unition

Glorification
When predicated of the Lord
Is the unition
Of His Human with the Divine.
To Glorify
Is to make Divine.

                         HD.300

Harm Is Done

No harm is done
When one person
Understands
The sense of the letter
In one way
And another in another way;
But harm is done
When falsities are brought in
Which are contrary
To Divine truths.

                              T.260

Precious

The church is such
As is the understanding
Of the Word in it:
Excellent and precious
If the understanding
Is from genuine truths
Out of the Word;
But destroyed
And even filthy
If from truths destroyed.

                              T.247

Through Conjunction

Man was created a native
Both of Heaven
And the world.
As a native of Heaven
He is spiritual,
As a native of the world
He is natural.
If therefore
Man becomes spiritual-rational
And also spiritual-moral
He is conjoined with God
And through that conjunction
He has salvation
And eternal life.

                              T.369

Shines with Splendor

Spiritual light
Which is the light
That goes forth from the Sun
Of the Spiritual World
Is in its essence
Truth;
Consequently in that World
Wherever truth appears
It shines with a splendor
Proportionate to its purity.

                              T.392

Lord Enters

Whenever lasciviousness
Is removed
Chastity enters;
Whenever intemperance
Is removed
Temperance enters;
Whenever deceit
Is removed
Sincerity enters
Whenever hatred
And the delight of revenge
Are removed
Love and the delight
Of love and friendship
Enter,
And so in other cases,
And this for the reason
That the Lord enters
And Heaven with Him.

E.790

Utterly Averse

They whose sins are remitted
Experience a delight
In worshipping God
For His own sake,
And in serving the neighbor
For the sake of the neighbor —
In doing good
For the sake of good,
And in speaking truth
For the sake of truth.
Such persons disclaim all merit
In the exercise
Of their charity and faith;
They are utterly averse
To all evils —
As enmity, hatred,
Revenge, adultery,
And not only do they shun them
But they abhor
The very thought of them.

HD.167

Paradisiac Scenes

The spiritual angels
Are clothed in garments
Of fine linen and silk —
Generally
In shining garments;
And as the spiritual Heavens
Correspond to the eyes
There are paradisiac scenes
Appearing in many places,
Rainbow-colored,
And these are
Of ineffable beauty,

E.831

No Longer from Self

By "good works" are meant
All things and every thing
That a man does
After he has turned away
From evils
Because they are sins
Against God;
For he then no longer
Does good works from self
But from the Lord.

E.837

Origin Appears

In this world
No one can determine
Whether works are
From the Lord or from man,
Since in external form
The two kinds
Appear the same,
And they can be distinguished
By the Lord alone;
But after man's life
In the world
Their origin is made evident.

E.794

Fully Receive

Only those who are
In the good of love
Have spiritual perception.
This is because
They receive Heavenly things
Not only with the hearing
But also with the love;
And to receive with the love
Is to receive fully.

E.8

Spoke from Divine

Those who are ignorant
Of the internal sense
Of the Word
May suppose
That the words
That the Lord spoke
Involve nothing more
Than what is obvious
In the sense of the letter,
When yet every particular
Of what the Lord spoke
Has a spiritual meaning;
For He spoke from the Divine,
And thus in the presence
Both of Heaven
And of the world.

E.163

"First Born"

By the "first-born"
Is not meant the first born
But the good
Of Heaven and the church
Because this is in first place;
And since all good in Heaven
Is from the Lord
He is called
The "First Born."

E.28

To Destroy Idolatries

Under the Lord's Providence
The Mohammedan Religion
Was raised up and adapted
To the genuis of the Orientals
To the end
That it might destroy
The idolatries of many nations
And give them some knowledge
Of the Lord
Before they entered
The Spiritual World.

P.255

Upward and Inward

Natural love
Is love of self and the world,
And spiritual love
Is love to the Lord
And love to the neighbor;
And love of self and the world
Looks downward and outward,
But love to the Lord
Looks upward and inward.

DLW.424

Preserved in Heaven

It is of the Lord's
Divine Providence
That the spiritual sense
Has been hidden
From the world
Until the present age,
And in the meanwhile
Has been preserved in Heaven
Among the angels
Who derive
Their wisdom from it.
That sense was known
To the ancients
Who lived before Moses
And was carefully studied.

P.264

Angels Sent

There are some Societies
That attend upon spirits
That are in the hells
And restrain them
From tormenting each other
Beyond prescribed limits,
And there are some
That attend upon those
Who are being raised
From the dead.
In general
Angels from each Society
Are sent to men
To watch over them
And to lead them away
From evil affections
And to inspire them
With good affections
So far as they will
Receive them in freedom.

H.391

To the Divine

Those think naturally
Who take account
Of the world only
And attribute all things
To nature
While those think spiritually
Who take account of Heaven
And attribute all things
To the Divine.

H.130

Consists of Truths

The genuine rational faculty
Consists of truths
And not falsities.
Whatever consists of falsities
Is not rational.

H.468

Not Nature

God from Eternity
Can be thought about
But in no wise
Nature from Eternity.
Consequently
The creation
Of the Universe by God
Can be thought about
But in no wise
Creation from nature.

P.51

Only by God

Who is not able
To understand
(If he will elevate
His mind a little)
That an Eternal life
Which is the lot
Of every man after death
Can be granted only
By an Eternal God?

T.32

Even Denies God

Those who have
Confirmed themselves
In favor of nature
Have brought
Such a state upon themselves
That they are no longer
Willing to raise their minds
Above nature;
Consequently
Their minds are shut above
And opened below.
Man thus becomes
Sensual-natural,
That is, spiritually dead;
At heart he even denies God.

DLW.162

Created Forms

Wisdom is not created
Neither is faith, nor truth,
Nor love, nor charity,
Nor good;
But forms for receiving these
Have been created
And these forms are
Human and angelic minds.

T.40

Shorten the Days

It is said in Matthew:
"Then shall be great tribulation
Such as hath not been
From the beginning of the world
Until now
No, nor ever shall be
And except those days
Should be shortened
No flesh would be saved."
This chapter treats
Of the consummation of the Age
By which the end
Of the present church is meant.
Therefore to "shorten those days"
Means to bring that church
To its end
And establish a new one.

T.182

Truths

God is Good itself
God is Good itself
And Truth itself,
And it was by means
Of Divine Truth
That He created the Universe;
And all the laws of order
By means of which
He preserves the Universe
Are truths . . .

T.87

Lusts Prevent

Anyone can see
That lusts
With their enjoyments
Block the way
And close the doors
Before the Lord
And that these
Cannot be cast out
By the Lord
So long as man himself
Holds the doors closed
And by pressing and pushing
From without
Prevents
Their being opened.

P.33

Spirit's Face

The face of a man's spirit
Differs greatly
From the face of his body.
The face of his body
Is from his parents
But the face of his spirit
Is from his affection
And is an image of it.

H.457

Divine-Human Union

The Lord's Glorification
Was also His state of union
With the Father.
He was in that state
When He was Transfigured
Before His three disciples
And also when
He wrought miracles
And whenever He said
That the Father and He
Are one.

T.104

Love and Wisdom

In relation to Spaces
God's Infinity is called
Immensity
But in relation to Times
God's Infinity is called
Eternity.
Also, His immensity
Means His Divinity
In respect to Love,
And eternity
His Divinity
In respect to Wisdom.

T.31

Human Face

Those that have been
In good affections
Appear with beautiful faces
But those that have been
In evil affections
With misshapen faces,
For man's spirit
Viewed in itself
Is nothing but his affection,
And the face
Is its outward form.

H.457

Sole Purpose

Of God's Divine Love
When He created the world
Was to conjoin man
To Himself
And Himself to man
That He might thus
Dwell with man.
This truth
The former churches
Did not possess.

T.786

Cloaks Evils

The merely natural man
Can see good and evil
In others;
But not having looked into
And examined himself
He does not see
Any evil in himself
And if any is discovered
By another
He cloaks it
As a serpent hides his head
In the dust
And immerses himself in it
As a hornet buries himself
In mud.

T.564

Perpetual Uses

The Universe
Consists
Of perpetual uses
Brought forth by Wisdom
But initiated
By Love.

T.47

No Weight

To worship as God
Some vicar on earth
Or to invoke as God
Some saint
Has no more weight
In Heaven
Than to make supplication
To the sun, moon, and stars
Or to ask for responses
For a diviner
And believe
What he puts forth,
Which is idle.

T.560

The Man Himself

Man is entirely
Of such a character
As is the ruling principle
Of his life;
It is this which distinguishes
One man from another;
And to this
The heaven of each individual
Is adapted
If he is a good man,
And his hell
If he is a wicked man;
It is this which constitutes
His very will,
His proper self,
And his peculiar nature;
For it is
The very *esse* of his life.
This cannot be
Changed after death
For it is
The man himself.

HD.57

Influx from God

The human soul
Being a superior
Spiritual substance
Receives influx
Immediately from God;
But the human mind
Being an inferior
Spiritual substance
Receives influx from God
Mediately
By the Spiritual World,
And the body
Being composed
Of the substances of nature
Receives influx from God
Mediately
By the natural world.

SB.8

Not Imputed

Falses of Religion
(If they do not
Disagree with good)
Do not produce evil
Except with those
Who are in evil.
Falses of Religion
Are not imputed
To those who are in good
But to those
Who are in evil.

HD.21

Church Is Such

It is not the Word
That constitutes the church
But the understanding of it,
And the church is such
As is the understanding
Of the Word
With those
Who are in the church.

T.243

Do Not Believe

Those in whom
The internal spiritual man
Is closed
Do not know
What the internal man is;
Neither do they believe
In the Word
Or in a life after death
Or in the things
Pertaining to Heaven;
And because they are
In merely natural light
They believe nature
To be from itself
And not from God.

T.410

Infinity

There are two properties
Of the natural world
Which cause all things
To be finite,
One is Space
The the other Time.
As the natural world
Was created by God,
And Space and Time
Were created together with it
And render it finite
It is necessary to think
Of the two origins
Of these properties —
Namely,
Immensity and Eternity,
For the immensity of God
Relates to Spaces
And His eternity
To Times,
While both
Immensity and eternity
Are included in Infinity.

T.27

His Sheepfold

The Lord God the Savior
Is to be approached
Because He is the God
Of Heaven and earth,
The Redeemer and Savior,
To whom omnipotence,
Omniscience,
Omnipresence,
Mercy itself,
And also justice
Belong;
Also because man
Is His creature
And the church
Is His sheepfold.

T.538

Evils Set Aside

The more fully
Evils in the natural man
Are set aside
By shunning them
And turning away from them
The more nearly is man
Conjoined with the Lord.

P.33

Tares

He that puts away
The evils of his will
By repentance
Is like one
Who in due time
Plucks up the tares
Sown in the field
By the devil
So that the seed
Implanted by the Lord God
Finds a clear soil
And grows up
To a harvest.

T.532

Turn to the Lord

All those
Who do good from Religion,
After death reject the doctrine
Of the present church
Respecting three Divine Persons
From Eternity
And also its faith
As applied to the three
In their order.
These turn
To the Lord God the Savior
And accept with pleasure
What belongs
To the New Church.

T.536

The Shining Word

In the shrines
Of the temples of Heaven
The Word shines
Before the eyes of the angels
Like a great star,
Sometimes like a sun;
And also from the bright
Radiance round about it,
There are seen as it were
Most beautiful rainbows.

T.209

Fallacies Dispersed

He who believes that man
Has a rational understanding
Before his natural
Has been purified from evils
Is deceived,
For the understanding
Consists in seeing
The truths of the church
From the light of Heaven;
And the light of Heaven
Does not flow
Into those not purified.
As the understanding
Is perfected
The falsities of Religion,
And of ignorance,
Are dispersed.

E.941

State of Children

The state of children
In the Other Life
Far surpasses
Their state in the world
For they are not clothed
With an earthly body
But with such a body
As the angels have.

H.331

Great Gulf

The Lord opened
A great gulf
Between the hells
And the Heavens
Which no one from the hells
Can cross.
If anyone attempts it,
At the first step
He is tortured
Like a serpent
Laid on a sheet of hot iron,
For at the first approach
Of the odor of Divine truth
The devils and satans
Instantly cast themselves
Into the abyss
And throw themselves
Into caves
And stop them up so closely
That not a crevice
Can be seen.

T.224

Above All

To love the Lord
Above all things
Consists solely
In doing no evil
To the Word
For the reason that the Lord
Is in the Word,
Or to the holy things
Of the church,
Or to the soul of anyone,
For the reason
That everyone's soul
Is in the Lord's hand.
Those who shun these evils
As monstrous sins
Love the Lord
Above all things.

P.94

Loves Evil

Those who give no thought
To the evils in themselves,
That is,
Do not examine themselves
And afterwards
Do not refrain
From their evils
Must needs be ignorant
Of what evil is
And must needs love it
From enjoyment,
For he who does not know
What evil is
Loves it.

P.101

Is in Truths

A man becomes spiritual
Only so far
As he is in truths,
For man is regenerated
Only by means of truths
And life in accordance
With them,
For by means of truths
He knows what life is.

P.84

Never Erased

Man has an external
And an internal memory
And every least thing
That a man has thought,
Willed, spoken, done,
Or even heard and seen
Is inscribed
On his internal
Or spiritual memory,
And what is there
Is never erased.

H.463

Two Freedoms

There is
Infernal freedom
And there is
Heavenly freedom
To think and will evil
And to speak and do it
As far as civil
And moral laws
Do not hinder
Is from infernal freedom.
But to think and will good
And to speak and do it
So far as opportunity
Is granted
Is from Heavenly freedom.

P.43

Still Alive

Nearly all
That go from this world
Are greatly surprised
To find they are still alive
And are just as much men
As before,
That they see, hear, and speak
And that their body enjoys
The sense of touch as before
With no difference whatever,
And when they cease to be
Astonished at themselves
They are astonished
That the church should know
Nothing about this state
Of men after death
And nothing
About Heaven and hell
When in fact
All that have ever lived
In the world
Are in the Other Life
And live as men.

H.456

Sin

No man
In the Christian world
Can be without
Recognition of sin
For every one
Is taught from infancy
What evil is
And from childhood
What the evil of sin is.
The evil of sin
Is no other than evil
Against the neighbor,
And evil against the neighbor
Is also evil against God,
Which is sin.

T.525

Faith Itself

Since Faith is from the Lord
And in the Lord
It may be said
That the Lord is Faith itself,
For its life and essence
Are in Him
And thus from Him.

T.347

In God's Hand

Who that has loved
His married partner
And his children
When they are dying or dead
Will not say within himself
That they are
In the hand of God
And that he shall
See them again
After his own death
And again be joined with them
In a life of love and joy?

CL.28

Angels See

The angels of Heaven can see
Whatever is done in hell
And what kind of monsters
Exist there,
While on the other hand
The spirits of hell
Can see nothing whatever
That is going on in Heaven;
They can no more
See the angels
Than if they were blind
Or were gazing
Into the empty air or ether.

T.61

Seem Talented

The avaricious,
Adulterous,
And crafty
Are especially sensual
Although to the world
They seem talented.
The interiors of their minds
Are vile and filthy;
By these they communicate
With the hells
And in the Word
They are called dead.

T.565

Love Reciprocal

Man is loved by the Lord
Just to the extent
That his will is formed
From good
And his understanding
From truth.
To be loved by the Lord
Is to love the Lord
Since love is reciprocal.

H.350

In God's Presence

To confess sins
Is to know evils,
To perceive them in oneself,
To charge oneself
With their guilt,
And to condemn oneself
On account of them.
When this is done
In the presence of God
It constitutes
The confession of sins.

HD.160

Idea of Three

They who entertain
(Respecting the Divinity)
An idea of Three Persons
Cannot at the same time
Have an idea of one God
For if they even *say*
That there is but one God
Still they *think* of Three.

HD.289

Forever Remains

The life of man
Cannot be changed
After death
But must forever remain
Such as it had been
In this world;
For the quality of man's spirit
Is in every respect the same
As that of his love;
And infernal love
Can never be transcribed
Into Heavenly love
Because they are
In direct opposition
To each other.

HD.239

Lord Plainly Teaches

The man who does not
Receive spiritual life —
That is,
Who is not born anew
By the Lord
Cannot enter Heaven.
This the Lord
Plainly teaches in John:
"Verily, verily,
I say unto thee,
Except a man be born again
He cannot see
The Kingdom of God."

HD.173

Would Be Consumed

No angel
Can ever be united
With the Divine itself
Except at a distance
And by means
Of a veil or covering
For otherwise
He would be consumed.

HD.304

Rejects

A man may know,
Think,
And understand much,
But when he is left
To solitary reflection
He rejects from himself
Everything
That is not in accordance
With his ruling love.
Hence also
He rejects such things
After the life of his body
When he lives as a spirit.

HD.113

Like Parent

Loving one's country
Is loving the public welfare,
One's country is the neighbor
Because it is
Like a parent
For one is born into it,
And it has nourished him
And continues to nourish him
And has protected
And continues to protect him
From injuries.

                                        T.414

Evidences

Any man is able
(If he will)
To find evidences
In favor of the Divine
In the visible things of nature
And this he does
Whenever he thinks of God
And of His omnipotence
In the creation
Of the Universe
And of His omnipresence
In the preservation of it.

                                        T.12

Among Hypocrites

Among consummate hypocrites
There is interior enmity
Against truly spiritual men,
For it is like that of satans
Against the angels
Of Heaven.
They are unconscious of this
While they are
Living in the world
But it manifests itself
After death.

                                        T.381

Born Spiritual

Man as to his soul
Is born spiritual
And is clothed
With what is natural
Which forms
His material body.
Therefore when his body
Is laid aside
His soul
(Clothed with a spiritual body)
Enters a world
Where all things are spiritual
And is there affiliated
With its like.

                                        T.583

Higher Neighbor

The church is the neighbor
That is to be loved
In a higher degree,
Thus even above
One's country
For the reason
That by his country
Man is initiated into civil life
But by the church
Into spiritual life.

                                        T.415

Loves All

He who loves
The Lord's Kingdom
Loves all
In the whole world
Who acknowledge the Lord
And have faith in Him
And charity
Towards the neighbor,
And he also
Loves all in Heaven.

                                        T.416

Defense Allowable

A good man
Is prudent and zealous
Only in defending,
And rarely
Prudent and zealous
In attacking.
It is the same
As with spirits of hell
And angels of Heaven;
The spirits of hell attack
And the angels of Heaven
Defend themselves.
From this
Comes the conclusion
That it is allowable
For any one
To defend his country
And his fellow citizens
Against invading armies.

P.252

Cleansing

That all cleansing
From evils
Is from the Lord
Is meant by this:
"If I wash thee not
Thou has no part
With me."

P.151

Useful and Beautiful

Before the angels
Every act or deed
Of a spiritual man
Is like a palatable fruit,
Useful and beautiful,
Which when opened and eaten
Yields flavor,
Use, and delight.

DLW.279

By Lord's Power

By means of temptations
The Lord
Glorified His Human
By His own power,
But men are regenerated
Not by their own power
But by the Lord.

E.893

His Works Are Good

When one shuns evils
Because they are opposed
To the Word,
And thus opposed to God,
And because they are from hell,
Then he lives
According to the laws
Of his Religion;
And so far as he lives
According to his Religion
He is led by the Lord,
And so far as he is led
By the Lord
His works are good.

E.825

Not Yet Known

All who are being regenerated
By the Lord
Undergo temptations,
And after these temptations
Experience joys.
But the source
Of the temptations
And of the joys that follow
Is not yet known in the world
For the reason
That there are few
Who are in knowledges
Of good and truth.

E.897

Light of Truth

I have often seen
Spiritual light
Which immensely exceeds
Natural light
In clearness and splendor,
For it is
As clearness and splendor
In their very essence;
It appears like
Resplendent and dazzling snow
Such as the garments of the Lord
When He was transfigured.
As light is Wisdom
Therefore the Lord
Calls Himself the Light
Which lightens every man,
And says in other places
That He is the Light, —
That is,
That He is Divine Truth.

SB.6

Through Man to God

The uses
Of all created things
Ascend by degrees to man
And through man
To God the Creator
From whom they are.

DLW.307

Perfected to Eternity

The angels assert
That by Wisdom from the Lord
They are being perfected
To Eternity,
Which also means
To Infinity,
Because Eternity
Is the Infinity of time.

CL.185

From Angel Lips

The angels wished
That I should declare
From their lips
That in the entire Heaven
There is not a single angel
Who was created such
From the beginning
Nor in hell any devil
Who was created an angel of light
And cast down;
But that all
Both in Heaven and in hell
Are from the Human Race.

H.311

Sinks Downward

Heaven consists
Of myriads of myriads
Of angels,
And unless all these
Looked to one God
They would fall away
From one another
And Heaven would be broken up.
Consequently,
If an angel of Heaven
But thinks of a plurality of gods
He is at once separated
And sinks downward.

DLW.25

In God

Love together with Wisdom
In its very essence
Is in God.
This no one can deny;
For God loves every one
From Love in Himself
And leads every one
From Wisdom in Himself.

DLW.29

Eternal Blindness

In creating the vast system
Called the Universe
God had a single end
In view
Which was
An Angelic Heaven
From the Human Race.
Whoever regards the world
As a work containing
Means to that end
Is able to look
Upon the created Universe
As a work coherent as a unit
And to see that the world
Is a complex of uses
Existing in a successive order
Looking to the Human Race
(From which is the Angelic Heaven)
As its end.
The Divine Love
Can be intent upon
No other end
Than the Eternal Blessedness
Of men;
And the Divine Wisdom
Can bring forth
Nothing but uses
That are means to that end.

T.13

Exalted

Beatitudes and pleasures
Are exalted
As the higher degrees
Of the mind
(Which are called
Spiritual and celestial)
Are opened in man;
And after his life
In the world
These degrees
Are enlarged to Eternity

P.37

Monsters

The angels of Heaven
Can see
Whatever is done in hell
And what kind of monsters
Exist there
While on the other hand
The spirits of hell
Can see nothing whatever
That is going on
In Heaven.

T.61

Resurrection

As soon as the
Heart's motion ceases
The man is resuscitated
But this is done
By the Lord alone.
Resuscitation means
The drawing forth of the spirit
From the body
And its introduction
Into the Spiritual World.
This is commonly called.
The Resurrection.

H.447

To Eternity

The operations
Of Divine Providence
Will continue to Eternity
Since every angel
Is perfecting in wisdom
To Eternity
But each
According to the degree
Of that affection
For good and truth
In which he was
When he left the world.

P.334

Renunciation

As regards
Renunciation of the world
It is the opinion of many
That to renounce the world
And to live in the spirit
And not in the flesh
Means to reject
All worldly concerns
Especially riches and honors;
To be continually engaged
In pious meditation
On God,
On Salvation,
And on eternal life;
To devote one's whole life
To prayer,
To the reading of the Word,
And the perusal of pious books;
And to suffer
Self-inflicted pain.
This however
Is not what is meant
By renouncing the world.
To renounce the world
Is to love God
And to love the neighbor;
And a man loves God
When he lives
According to His commandments;
And he loves the neighbor
When he performs uses.
In order therefore
That a man may receive
The life of Heaven
It is necessary that he should
Live in the world
And engage in the various
Offices and businesses of life.
A life of abstraction
From secular concerns
Is a life of thought and faith
Separate from a life
Of love and charity.

HD.126

Eternal

All things pertaining to man
Are temporal
And for this reason
May be called temporal;
While all things
Pertaining to the Lord
Are eternal,
And for this reason
The Lord is called Eternal.

P.218

Limitless Varieties

Love is manifold,
So manifold
That its varieties
Are limitless,
As can be seen
From the Human Race
On the earths
And in the Heavens.
There is no man or angel
So like another
That there is no difference.
Love is what distinguishes.

DLW.368

Barren Ground

When the children of Israel
Lived
According to the Commandments,
The earth yielded its increase;
Likewise the flocks and herds;
But when they lived
Contrary to the Commandments
The ground was barren
And accursed;
Instead of harvests
It yielded thorns and briars;
The flocks and herds miscarried;
And wild beasts broke in.

DLW.345

First Cause

All things in the Universe
Which are according
To Divine order
Have relation
To good and truth;
There is nothing
Either in Heaven or on earth
Which has not relation
To these two;
The reason is
Because both good and truth
Proceed
From the Divine Being
Who is
The First Cause of all.

HD.11

Adheres

Care should be taken
That falses of Religion
Be not confirmed
Because a persuasion
Of what is false
Arises thence
Which adheres to man
After death.

HD.21

Also The Church

As all things of Heaven
Have relation
To good and truth
So also
Have all things
Of the church
Because the good and truth
Of Heaven
Are also
The good of truth
Of the church.

HD.12

Perverted Beliefs

No one who
(From confirmation and life)
Is principled in evil
And thence in falsity
Can know
What good and truth are,
For he believes
His own evil to be good
And his falsity
To be truth.

HD.19

Expanses

The Ancient Heavens
Constitute superior expanses
While the new Heaven
Constitutes an expanse
Beneath them
For the Heavens are expanses
Above one another.

HD.4

Fountains

There are two loves
From which
As from their very fountain
All goods and truths spring;
And there are two loves
From which
All evils and falsities spring.
The two loves
From which are all
Goods and truths
Are love to the Lord
And love towards the neighbor,
While the two loves
From which
Are all evils and falsities.
Are love of self
And love of the world.

T.399

Stands Immovable

That in the Spiritual World
There is a Sun
Different from that
In the natural world
I am able to testify
For I have seen it;
In appearance
It is a globe of fire
Like our sun;
It is of much the same magnitude
And at the same distance
From the angels
As our sun is from men,
But it does not rise or set
But stands immovable
In a middle altitude
Between the zenith
And the horizon
Whence the angels enjoy
Perpetual light
And perpetual spring.

SB.4

Spiritual Substance

There is only one substance
From which all things are,
And the Sun
Of the Spiritual World
Is that spiritual substance.

DLW.300

By Enjoyable Things

In the Spiritual World
All children
Are led by the Lord
Into angelic wisdom
And through that
Into Heavenly love
By means of things
Enjoyable and pleasing.

P.136

Examine Spirit

One cannot be reformed
Unless the evils
Of his spirit
Are examined;
For after death
Man lives a spirit,
And all the evils
That are in the spirit
Remain.
The spirit is examined
Only by man's
Attending to his thoughts,
Especially his purposes.

P.152

Heartbeats

When questioned
The angels declared
That they are just as much men
As those in the world
And possess a body
As well as they,
But a spiritual body,
And feel the beat
Of the heart in the chest,
And the beat of the arteries
In the wrist,
Just as men do
In the natural world.

DLW.391

Shuts in Evils

Compelled worship
Shuts in evils;
And evils then lie hidden
Like fire in wood under ashes
Which is continually
Kindling and spreading
Till it breaks out
In flames.

P.136

Think from Religion

Those who do not
Think from Religion
Do not have conscience
Because they are not spiritual;
Consequently,
If external bonds,
Which are fears respecting
The law and reputation,
Should be removed from them
They would rush
Into every wickedness;
While on the other hand
If external bonds,
Which are fears respecting
The law and reputation,
Should be taken away
From those who think
From Religion,
They would still act
Sincerely, justly, and well;
For they fear God
And are kept in a life
Of obedience and charity.

E.107

Life of His Love

"Life" signifies the Lord
And therefore
Salvation and Heaven
Because everything of life
Is from one only Fountain,
And that only Fountain
Of life is the Lord,
While angels and men
Are merely forms
Receiving life from Him.
The life itself
That goes forth
From the Lord
And fills
Heaven and the world
Is the Life of His love.

E.186

On a Mountain

No one
So long as he is in evil
Can see good,
But he who is in good
Can see evil.
Evil is below
As in a cave,
Good is above
As on a mountain.

DLW.271

Form of Wisdom

The form of wisdom,
Is man;
And because man
Is the form of wisdom,
He is also the form
Of love, mercy, clemency,
Good, and truth,
Because these make one
With wisdom.

DLW.286

Steadfast

To "overcome" is to resist
Evils and falsities
And to tame and subdue them
As one's enemies;
But no one overcomes
Unless he is steadfast
In spiritual affection for truth
Even to the end
Of his life in the world;
The work is then finished,
For man remains to Eternity
Such as he then is —
Namely,
Such as his life has been
Up to that point;
Death is what completes it.

E.128

Interiors Elevated

The moral life
Of those who are spiritual
Is a truly moral life,
For these,
When they think in spirit —
That is,
When they are thinking
Secretly by themselves,
Do not think
From self and the world
But from the Lord
And Heaven.
For the interiors
Of their minds
Are actually elevated
By the Lord into Heaven
And are there conjoined
To Him.

E.182

Life of Self

He who loves himself
Above all things
Is mindful of himself
In every least thing;
He thinks about himself,
Acts in his own behalf;
For his life
Is the life of self.

T.399

No Higher Joy

Every one
Who comes into Heaven
Enters into the highest joy
Of his heart;
He can bear no higher joy,
For he would be
Suffocated thereby.

P.254

Blaze and Glisten

As the garments of angels
Correspond to their intelligence
They correspond also
To truth
Since all intelligence
Is from Divine truth;
And therefore it is the same
Whether you say
That angels are clothed
In accordance with intelligence
Or in accordance
With Divine truth.
The garments of some
Blaze as if with flame,
And those of others
Glisten as if with light,
Because flame
Corresponds to good,
And light to truth.

H.179

Spiritual Death

Spiritual death
Is turning away
And removal
From the Lord.
When evil spirits
Enter any angelic Society —
Because the Divine of the Lord
Is there present —
They are direfully tormented
And not only turn away
But even cast themselves
Down into the depths
Where no light enters;
Some into
Dark caverns of rocks;
In a word, into the hells.
This turning away
And removal from the Lord
Is called spiritual death.

HE.78

Heavenly Form

The form of Heaven
Is the form
Of all the affections
Of the Divine Love there.
That form is composed
Of myriads and myriads;
And myriads enter it
Each year
And will continue
To enter into it to Eternity.
All children enter into it
And as many adults
As are affections
From a good of love.

P.63

Never the Same

In the entire Heaven
There are no two angels
Or no two spirits
That are wholly the same
Nor can there be
To Eternity.

P.56

Two Essentials

There are two things
That are at once
The essentials
And the universals
Of Religion
Namely,
Acknowledgment of God
And repentance.
These two
Are void of meaning
To those who believe
That men are saved
Out of mere mercy
Howsoever they live.

P.340

Ever Present

God is present
In space without space
And in time without time
Because He is always
The same
From Eternity to Eternity
Thus He is the same
Since the world was created
As before.

T.30

Precious Stones

Precious stones
Exist in the Spiritual World
As well as
In the natural world,
And their spiritual origin
Is the truth of the sense
Of the letter of the Word.
This seems incredible
And yet it is true
And this is why
Precious stones
Are so frequently mentioned
In the Word.

T.217

Clear as Day

Let no one believe
That there is anything
That a man has ever
Thought in himself
Or done in secret
That can be concealed
After death
But let him believe
That all things
And each single thing
Are then made
As clear as day.

H.463

Hands of Jehovah

The Divine
Is in each and every thing
Of the created Universe.
Consequently
The created Universe
Is the work
Of the "hands of Jehovah"
As is said in the Word —
That is,
The work of Divine Love
And Divine Wisdom,
For these are meant
By the "hands of Jehovah."

DLW.59

Foundation

Heaven is in conjugial love;
And the natural man
Whose conjugial love
Derives its pleasures
Only from the flesh
Cannot approach to Heaven
Nor to any angel
No, nor to any man
Principled in this love,
It being the foundation
Of all celestial
And spiritual loves.

CL.71

Few Drops

No one is wise from himself
But only from the Lord.
For the things
In which a man is wise
Compared with the things
In which he is not wise
Are as a few drops of water
Compared
To a great lake.

P.36

No One

No one can be admitted
Into the delight of Heaven
(Which is commonly called
Heavenly joy)
Who is in the delight
Of hell
Or (what is the same)
No one who is in
The delight of evil
Can be admitted
Into the delight of good.

P.338

Love Remains

After death
Conjugial love remains
With those
Who go to Heaven
Which is the case
With all those who become
Spiritual
Here on earth.

CL.38

Man's Only Refuge

If one lives for a time
With robbers and pirates
He finally becomes like them;
Or if one lives
With adulterers and harlots
He soon thinks
Nothing of adultery;
For all evils are contagious
And may be compared
To a pestilence.
The delights of evil
Into which every man is born
Are the cause.
The only refuge from destruction
For anyone is the Lord.

T.120

Clouds of Heaven

It is written in many places
That the Lord will come
In the clouds of heaven,
And as no one
Has hitherto known
What is meant by
"Clouds of heaven"
It has been believed
That the Lord
Would appear in them
In Person.
Heretofore
It has not been known
That "the clouds of heaven"
Mean the Word
In the sense of the letter
And that
The "glory and power"
In which He is to come
Mean the spiritual sense
Of the Word.

T.776

Cannot Be Changed

The male principle
In the male
Is male
In every part of his body
Even the most minute
And also
In every idea of his thought
And every spark
Of his affection.
The same is true
Of the female principle
In the female;
And since of consequence
The one cannot be changed
Into the other
It follows that after death
A male is a male
And a female, a female.

CL.33

Present to Himself

There is no need for man
To enumerate his sins
Before the Lord
Nor to supplicate
Forgiveness of them.
He need not enumerate them
If he has searched them out
And seen them
In himself;
Consequently
They are present to the Lord
Because they are
Present to himself.

T.539

Roots Grow

Man can repent of evils
That he has done
In the body
And still think and will evil;
But this is like cutting off
The trunk of a bad tree
And leaving its root
In the ground
From which the same bad tree
Grows up again
And spreads forth
It branches.

T.532

Affects Everyone

The nature of Divine Love
Is known from its sphere
Which pervades the Universe
And affects every one
In accordance with his state.
It especially affects parents
And is the source
Of their love
For their children.

T.44

Funeral Services

I have talked with some
Two days after their decease
And have told them
That their funeral services
Were then being held
And preparations made
For their interment;
To which they replied
That it was well to cast aside
That which had served them
As a body
And for bodily functions
In the world;
And they wished me to say
That they were not dead
But living as men
The same as before,
And had merely migrated
From one world
Into the other.

                                    H.312

Creator and Upholder

Spiritual existences
Are derived from a Sun
Which is pure Love
In the midst of which
Is the Creator and Upholder
Of the Universe,
Jehovah God.

                                    SB.9

Even False

Truths not genuine
(and even falses)
May be consociated
With genuine truths
With those who are in good
But not with those
Who are in evil.

                                    HD.21

Effected Salvation

The Lord effected salvation
By the subjugation
Of the hells
Which infested every man
Coming into the world
And going out of the world
And at the same time
By the Glorification
Of His Humanity.

                                    HD.293

Innumerable

The delights of Heaven
Are ineffable and innumerable
But he that is in
The mere delight
Of the body or of the flesh
Can have no knowledge of
(Or belief in)
A single one
Of these innumerable delights.

                                    H.398

Noble to Die

That one's country
Should be loved
Not as one loves himself
But more than himself
Is a law inscribed
On the human heart
From which has come
The well-known principle
(Which every true man endorses)
That if the country
Is threatened with ruin
From an enemy
Or any other source
It is noble
To die for it
And glorious for a soldier
To shed his blood for it.

                                    T.414

Angelic Power

So great is the power
Of angels
In the Spiritual World
That if I should make known
All that I have witnessed
In regard to it,
It would exceed belief.
Any obstruction there
That ought to be removed
Because it is contrary
To Divine order
The angels cast down or overthrow
Merely by an effort of the will
And a look.
Thus I have seen mountains
That were occupied by the evil
Cast down and overthrown
And sometimes shaken
From end to end
As in earthquakes;
Also rocks cleft asunder
To their bottoms,
And the evils who were upon them
Swallowed up.
I have seen also
Hundreds of thousands
Of evil spirits
Dispersed by angels
And cast down into hell.
Numbers
Are of no avail
Against them;
Neither are devices,
Cunning, or combination,
For they see through them all
And disperse them
In a moment.
Such power do angels have
In the Spiritual World.
But it must be understood
That the angels have no power
From themselves
But all their power
Is from the Lord.

H.229

All Religion Teaches

The common Religion
Of the whole Christian world
Teaches that man
Must examine himself,
See his sins,
Acknowledge them,
Confess them before God,
And refrain from them;
And that this is repentance,
Remission of sins,
And consequent salvation.

P.127

Persuasive Faith

Faith induced by miracles
Is not faith but persuasion
For there is nothing
Rational in it,
Still less anything spiritual.
For it is only
An external
Without an internal.
The same is true
Of everything that a man does
From such a persuasive faith.

P.131

Sight and Reason

What the Lord teaches
He gives to man
The ability to perceive
Rationally,
And this in two ways:
In one
Man sees in himself
That a thing is true
As soon as he hears it,
In the other
He understands it
By means of reasons.

P.150

Highest Seat

Religion alone
Renews and regenerates man.
Religion
Occupies the highest seat
In the human mind
And sees beneath it
The civil matters
Pertaining to the world;
It also ascends
By means of them
As the pure sap
Ascends through a tree
To its very top.

T.601

Perpetual Creation

"By the Word of Jehovah
Where the Heavens made."
The "Word" means
The Divine Truth.
As the Universe was created
By this Truth
So also
Was the Universe
Preserved by it;
For as subsistence
Is perpetual existence
So preservation
Is perpetual creation.

T.224

Lamps Lighted

By means of doctrine
Not only is the Word
Understood:
It also shines
In the understanding,
Since it then becomes
Like a candelabrum
With its lamps lighted.

T.227

Man's Spirit

Man's spirit
Is in every least thing
That takes place in the body
And it is that
Which impels the natural
To do
Whatever it does;
The natural
Viewed in itself
Is passive
Or a dead force,
But the spiritual
Is active
Or is a living force.

T.607

Unless a New Church

Unless a new church
Shall be raised up
In place of the present one
"No flesh can be saved"
According to the Lord's words
In Matthew's Gospel.

T.758

Sticks Fast

When self and the world
Are ends,
The mind
In reading the Word
Sticks fast
In self and the world
And in consequence
Their thought is always
From what is their own;
And man's own
Is in darkness
Respecting everything
That pertains
To Heaven and the church.

T.233

All Are Taught

All in the Spiritual World
Are taught and led
By the Lord
By means of angels,
And as they then know
That they are living
After death
And that there is
A Heaven and a hell
They at first receive truths;
But those who in the world
Did not acknowledge God
And shun evils as sins
Soon weary of truths
And withdraw.

P.328

Man's Mind

Man's mind is his spirit,
And the spirit is the man,
While the body
Is an external
By means of which
The mind of spirit
Feels and acts
In the world.

DLW.386

Many Inquiries

Many in the learned world
Have wearied themselves
With inquiries
Respecting the soul;
But as they knew nothing
Of the Spiritual World,
Or of man's state
After death
They could only frame theories —
Of the nature of the soul
They could have no idea.

DLW.394

Forever Enlarged

The inifinite and eternal
That the Lord looks to
In forming His Heaven
Out of men
Is that it shall be enlarged
To Infinity and to Eternity,
And that He may thus
Have a constant
Abiding place
In the end of His creation.

P.202

With Inmost Heaven

Hell is called adultery;
And Heaven on the other hand
Is called marriage;
Moreover,
The love of adultery
Communicates
With the lowest hell
While love truly conjugial
Communicates
With the inmost Heaven.

P.144

His Dwelling Place

That God is in man
And that He makes
His abode with him
Is known from the Word
For which reason
It is customary
For preachers to declare
That men
Ought to prepare themselves
To receive God
That he may enter into them
And be in their hearts,
That they may be
His dwelling place.

DLW.359

Radiant Bells

How great the Divine Love is,
And what it is,
Can be seen by comparison
With the sun of the world
In its greatest ardor;
It is (if you will believe it)
Much more ardent
Than the sun.
For this reason
The Lord as a Sun
Does not flow without mediums
Into the Heavens,
But the ardor of His Love
Is gradually tempered
On the way.
These temperings appear
As radiant belts
About the Sun;
Furthermore,
The angels are veiled
With a thin adapting cloud
To prevent their being harmed
By the inflowing Love.

H.120

Receives in Heart

To "overcome"
Is to receive in the heart
Because every one
Who is to receive
Spiritual life
Must fight
Against evils and falsities
Which belong
To his natural life;
And when he overcomes them
He receives in the heart
Goods and truths which belong
To the spiritual life.
To "receive in the heart"
Is to receive
In the will and love.

E.109

Not Formless Minds

Good spirits
With whom I have spoken
Are deeply grieved
At the ignorance
In the church
About the condition of Heaven
And of spirits and angels;
And in their displeasure
They charged me
To declare positively
That they are not
Formless minds
Nor ethereal breaths
But are men in very form
And see, hear, and feel
As fully as those
Who are in the world.

H.77

Nothing But Craft

Moral life
From love of self
And the world
Is not in itself moral,
Although it seems to be moral,
For man then acts rightly,
Sincerely, and justly
For the sake
Of self and the world;
And the good,
Sincere, and just
Serve him
As means to an end,
Which is either
That he may be raised
Above others
And rule over them
Or that he may gain swealth;
Therefore such a life
Regarded in itself
Is nothing
But craft and fraud.

E.182

Divine Foresight

Divine foresight
Is in the most
Particular things
From Eternity,
And Divine Providence
Is in the most
Particular things
To Eternity;
Consequently,
Whatsoever proceeds
From the Lord
Is from Eternity
To Eternity.

E.23

Increase of Wisdom

Conjugial love enters
According to the increase
Of wisdom,
Which is
According to the implantation
Of the church
From the Lord

CL.141

Mind Opened

The spiritual mind
Is chiefly opened
By man's abstaining
From doing evils
Because they are contrary
To the
Divine Commandments
In the Word.
If man
Abstains from evils
From any other fear
Than this,
His spiritual mind
Is not opened.

E.790

Divine Source

In the created Universe
And in each of its particulars
There is a marriage
Of good and truth;
And this is so
Because good is of Love
And truth is of Wisdom,
And these two
Are in the Lord;
And out of Him
All things were created.

DLW.402

Is the Word

The Word
Is from the Lord
And consequently
The Lord
Is in the Word
Even to the extent
That He is the Word;
For the Word
Is Divine Truth
Which is solely
From the Lord.

E.790

False Belief

It is believed in the world
That man has life
Implanted in him by birth
And that it does not therefore
Flow in unceasingly
From the Lord
Who alone has life in Himself
And who thus alone
Is life.
But this belief
Is a belief
In what is false.

E.82

In Divine Truths

From Divine Love
Divine good goes forth
And Divine good is received
By angels and men
In Divine truths.

H.371

Kingdom of Uses

With all in the Heavens
Goods are goods in act
Which are uses.
Everyone there
Performs a use,
For the Lord's Kingdom
Is a Kingdom of uses.

H.387

Still Remain

Many are not aware
That they are in evils
Because they do not do them
Since they fear
The civil laws
And the loss of reputation
And thus from custom
And habit
Fall into the way
Of shunning evils
As detrimental
To their honor and success.
But when evils
Are not shunned
From a religious principle
On the ground
That they are sins
And antagonistic to God
The lusts of evil
Still remain
Like impure waters
Confined and stagnant.

P.117

Falls to Nothing

Everyone has a general idea
That Angels
Are in the human form
And have homes
Which are called
The mansions of Heaven
Which surpasses in magnificence
All earthly dwellings;
But this general idea
(Which flows in from Heaven)
At once falls to nothing
When it is brought under direct
Scrutiny and inquiry
Whether it is so
As happens especially
With the learned.

H.183

Continual Increase

The advance of the delights
Of marriage love towards Heaven
Is into states
Of blessedness and happiness
Continually increasing
Until they become
Innumerable and ineffable.

H.386

Grief to Angels

It is a great grief
To the angels
That learned men
For most part
Ascribe all things to nature
And have thereby so closed up
The interiors of their minds
As to be unable to see
Anything of truth
From the light of truth
Which is the light
Of Heaven.

H.464

Heaven Removed

Heaven in removed from man
When the Lord and His Divine
Are denied,
As was done
By the Parasees
Who said that the Lord
Wrought miracles
By Beelzebub
And had an unclean spirit.

E.778

Even By Steps

Angels of the third Heaven
Know what a man is
By the tone of his speech,
Also by his step,
By the touch of the hand,
By the action of his body,
And by many other things
Which are acts.

E.839

Little or Great

By works
All things are meant
That a man does,
Speaks, or writes,
Whether great and many
Or little and few;
As whatever an officer does
In his office,
Or whatever a priest
Does in his,
Or a servant in his;
All such works
Whether little or great
Are good
When they are done
From the Lord in man.

E.839

Only From God

It is commanded in the Word
That man
Must not commit adultery,
Must not steal,
Must not kill,
Must not bear false witness,
It is known that man
Is able to do
All these things of himself,
Also that his is able
To refrain from them
Because they are sins;
And yet he is not able
To refrain from them
From himself
But only from God.

E.802

Everything of Religion

And everything of the church
Has regard to the Divine,
To Heaven,
And to spiritual life;
And these can be conjoined
With no other
With no other
Than a spiritual love.

E.817

Good Itself

Whatever a man does
From chastity itself,
From honesty itself,
From charity itself;
From truth itself,
From justice itself
(As if from himself)
He does from God,
And consequently,
They are good itself.

E.802

Unceasingly

The Lord is unceasingly
In the act
Of regenerating man
Because He is unceasingly
In the act of saving him,
And no one
Can be saved
Unless he is regenerated,
According to the Lord's
Own words in John:
"Except a man be born again
He cannot not see
The Kingdom of God."

                                        T.577

However Numerous

However numerous
Truths are,
And however diverse
They appear,
They make one from the Lord
Who is the Word,
The God of Heaven and earth,
The God of all flesh,
The God of the church,
The God of light and truth,
The God of life eternal.

                                        T.349

In Heaven's Light

The brightness and splendor
Of the light of Heaven
Are such
As cannot be described.
All things
That I have seen
In the Heavens
Have been in that light
Thus more clearly and distinctly
Than things in this world.

                                        H.126

Regenerated Differently

Every man may be regenerated
Each according to his state,
For the simple and the learned
Are regenerated differently,
As are those engaged
In different pursuits
And those who fill
Different offices;
Those who search
Into the external things
Of the Word
And those who search
Into its internals;
Those who are principled
In natural good from parents
And those who are in evil;
Those who from their infancy
Have entered into
The vanities of the world
And those who sooner or later
Have withdrawn from them —
In a word,
Those who constitute
The Lord's external church
Are regenerated differently
From those who constitute
His internal church;
And this variety
Like that of men's
Features and dispositions,
Is infinite
And yet every one
(According to his state)
May be regenerated and saved.

                                        T.580

By Means

By means of sensual things
Man communicates
With the world
And by means of rational things
With Heaven.

                                        T.565

Lord's Divine Body

The Lord rose again
Not as to his spirit alone
But also as to his body
Because when He was
In the world
He Glorified His whole Human —
That is,
Made it Divine;
For his soul,
Which He had from the Father,
Was of itself the very Divine.
While His body became
A likeness of the soul —
That is,
Of the Father,
Thus also Divine.

H.316

To Love Truths

To love truths
From spiritual affection
Is to love
What is just and equitable
Because it is just and equitable,
What is honest and right
Because it is honest and right,
And what is good and true
Because it is good and true.

H.468

See the Divinity

All who are really
Members of the church
And enlightened
By the light of Heaven
See the Divinity in the Lord,
But they
Who are not thus enlightened
Can see in Him
Nothing but the humanity.

HD.285

Rich and Poor

The rich and the poor alike
Come into Heaven
The one as easily
As the other.
The belief that the poor
Enter Heaven easily
And the rich with difficulty
Comes from a wrong
Understanding of the Word.

H.365

Equally Capable

Angelic minds
And human minds
Are the same
Both enjoying the ability
To understand,
Perceive, and will,
And both formed
To receive Heaven;
For the human mind
Is just as capable
Of becoming wise
As the angelic mind.

H.314

Heavenly Country

It should be known
That those
Who love their country
And render
Good service to it
From good will,
After death
Love the Lord's Kingdom;
For then
That is their country,
And those
Who love the Lord's Kingdom
Love the Lord Himself.

T.414

Jehovah

The name Jehovah
Which the Lord restored
Signifies the supreme
And only Being,
The Source of everything
That is or exists
In the Universe.
Jove,
A name derived
Possibly from Jehovah,
Was worshipped
As a supreme god
By the heathen;
And many other gods
Who composed his court
They also clothed with divinity;
While in the following Age
Wise men
Like Plato and Aristotle
Confessed that these
Were not gods
But were so many
Properties, qualities,
And attributes
Of the one God,
Being called gods
Because there was
Something Divine
In each of them.

T.9

God's Leading

Everyone must confess
That to be led by good
Is freedom
And to be led by evil
Is slavery;
Because to be led by good
Is to be led
By the Lord,
And to be led by evil
Is to be led
By the devil.   P.43

All from God

All the good
And all the truth
That anyone has
Is from the Lord
And not from himself;
And no one
Can even mention the Lord
(Or His names
"Jesus" and "Christ")
Except from Him.

P.53

Rich in Heaven

The rich enter Heaven
Just as easily as the poor
And no man
Is shut out of Heaven
On account of his wealth
Or received into Heaven
On account of his poverty.
Both the rich and the poor
Are in Heaven
And many of the rich
In greater glory and happiness
Than the poor.

H.357

When Children Die

When children die
They are still children
In the Other Life
Having a like infantile mind,
A like innocence in ignorance,
And a like tenderness
In all things.
They are only in the rudiments
Of a capacity
To become angels
For children are not angels
But become angels.

H.330

Deeds of Charity

There were some spirits
Who thought themselves
Better instructed than others
And who said
That they had believed
In the world
That Heavenly joy
Would consist solely
In praising and giving glory
To God,
And that this would be
Their active life.
These were told that praising
And giving glory to God
Is not a proper active life,
And that God has no need
Of praises and glorification,
But it is His will instead
That they should perform uses,
And thus the good works
That are called
Deeds of charity.

H.404

Accommodated

As the Word
Is a revelation from God
It is Divine
In all its parts
And in every particular;
For what proceeds from God
Cannot be otherwise.
That which proceeds from God
Descends through the Heavens
Down to man;
Wherefore in the Heavens
It is accommodated
To the wisdom of the angels
Who are there.
And on earth
It is accommodated
To the apprehension of man.

HD.252

Loves His Country

The man who loves his country
And does good to it
From a principle of benevolence,
When he comes into the Other Life
Loves the Kingdom of the Lord;
For in that life
The Kingdom of the Lord
In his country;
And he who loves
The Kingdom of the Lord
Loves the Lord Himself;
For the Lord is all in all
In His Kingdom.

HD.93

Matters of Life

Essential Divine worship
In the Heavens
Does not consist
In going to church
And hearing preaching
But in a life
Of love, charity, and faith
In accordance with doctrine;
Preachings in churches
Serve solely
As means of instruction
In matters of life.

H.222

Indivisible

God is one,
Indivisible,
And the same
From Eternity to Eternity,
Not the same simply
But infinitely the same.
All variableness
Is in the subjects
In which He dwells.

T.366

Free Worship

Worship not compelled
(When it is genuine)
Is spiritual, living,
Clear, joyful:
Spiritual
Because there is spirit
From the Lord in it,
Living
Because there is life
From the Lord in it,
Clear
Because there is wisdom
From the Lord in it,
And joyful
Because there is Heaven.
From the Lord in it.

P.137

Appropriated

Nothing is appropriated
To man
Except what he does
From freedom
In accordance
With reason.

P.138

By Lord Alone

For several years
I have talked
With spirits and angels;
Nor has any spirit dared
(Or any angel wished)
To instruct me
About any matter
In the Word,
Or about any matter
Of doctrine from the Word;
But I have been taught
By the Lord alone.

P.135

See More Clearly

Many of the learned
Who have thought much,
And especially
Who have written much,
Have weakened and obscured
(Yea, have destroyed)
Their common perception;
While the simple
See more clearly
What is good and true
Than those who think themselves
Their superiors in wisdom.

DLW.361

Doing Uses

By Uses
Goods are meant;
And therefore
Doing uses
Means doing goods;
And doing uses or goods
Means serving others
And ministering to them.

P.215

Last State Worse

He who returns to his evils
After he has worshipped
Profanes
The goods and truths
Of worship;
And the lot after death
Of those who commit
Profanation
Is the worst of all.
Such as these are meant
By the Lord's words
That their last state
Becomes worse
Than their first.

P.133

Would Perish

Man's own prudence
Is continually
Raising its head,
And Divine Providence
Is continually
Putting it down;
If man felt this
He would be provoked
And enraged against God
And would perish;
But as long
As he does not feel it
He may be provoked
And enraged with men
And with himself
(And also with fortune)
But this does not
Destroy him.

P.211

Beautiful Angels

All in the Spiritual World
Are forms of their own love —
The angels
Forms of Heavenly love,
The devils of hellish love;
The devil deformed
In face and body,
But the angels
Beautiful.

DLW.369

Performs Uses

When the love of Heaven
Is inwardly
In the love of the world
And through this
In the love of self
Man from the God of Heaven
Performs uses in each.

T.395

Everywhere Shown

In treating of Heaven
It has been everywhere shown
That the God of Heaven
Is the Lord,
Thus that the whole
Government of the Heavens
Is the Lord's government.

H.536

Purest Delight

The delight of marriage
Which is a purer
And more exquisite
Delight of touch,
Transcends all the rest
Because of its use,
Which is the procreation
Of the Human Race
And thereby
Of the angels of Heaven.

H.402

To End of Life

When a man
Has examined himself,
Acknowledged his sins,
And done the work of repentance,
He must continue
(Steadfastly perservering)
In the practice of what is good
Even to the end of his life;
For should he afterwards relapse
Into his former life
And embrace it
He becomes guilty
Of profanation,
Since he then conjoins
Evil with good
And his latter state
Becomes worse than the first.

HD.169

Male and Female

Since man lives as man
After death,
And man is male and female
And there is
Such a distinction
Between the male principle
And the female principle
That the one
Cannot be changed
Into the other
It follows that after death
The males lives a male
And the female a female.

CL.32

Can Be Continued

The spiritual man
Can think of God
And perceive such things
As are of God;
He can also love God
And be affected
By what is from God;
From which it follows
That he is capable
Of conjunction with God

T.369

Complete Victory

The last temptation
Of the Lord
Was in the
Garden of Gethsemane
And upon the Cross
At which time He gained
A complete victory
By which He
Subjugated the hells
And at the same time
Glorified His human.

HD.302

Purely Cold

He who acknowledges
The Lord
But sets charity aside
Acknowledges Him
With the lips only;
His acknowledgment
Is purely cold
Within which
There is no faith
For it lacks
Spiritual essence.

T.367

Both from the Lord

Since all willing
Is from love
And all understanding
From wisdom
It follows
That the power to will
Must be from Divine Love
And power to understand
From Divine Wisdom
And thus both must be
From the Lord
Who is Divine Love itself
And Divine Wisdom itself.

P.89

Dwells in Darkness

Evil dwells in darkness
And faith in light;
And evil
By means of falsities
Extinguishes faith,
As darkness
Extinguishes light.
Evil is black like ink
While faith is white
Like snow.

T.383

Lord's Second Coming

The Coming of the Lord
Which is His Second Coming
Is taking place
In order that the evil
May be separated
From the good
And that those
Who have believed
(And do believe) in Him
May be saved,
And that from them
A new angelic Heaven
And a new church on earth
May be formed,
And without this
No flesh could be saved.

T.772

Lord Provides

The Lord provides
That everyone
Who acknowledges God
And refrains from doing evils
Because they are
Sins against God
Should have a place
In Heaven.

P.326

Ineffable Wisdom

No one can come
Into the ineffable wisdom
Of the angels
Except through conjunction
With the Lord
And in the measure
Of that conjunction;
For the Lord alone
Opens the spiritual degree
And the celestial degree.

P.34

From the Lord

It is not from the angels
But from the Lord
That Heaven is Heaven;
For the love and wisdom
In which angels are
And which make Heaven
Are not from the angels
But from the Lord
And in fact
Are the Lord in them.

P.28

Life from God

In man
The Lord alone is active
And man of himself
Is merely passive
And it is by influx
Of life from God
That man is also active.
It is because this influx
Of life from God
Is unceasing
That it seems to man
As if he were active
From himself.

T.110

Way to Heaven

If you have Religion
You will see
That repentance from sins
Is the way to Heaven
And that faith
Separate from repentance
Is not faith
And that those
Who are not in faith
Because they do not repent
Are in the way to hell.

P.114

Great Absurdities

Many great absurdities
Have crept
Into the minds of men
(And thus into the church)
Through the heads of reformers
From their not understanding
The order in which
God created the Universe
And each and all things in it.

T.52

Not Accepted

Those who do good
From natural goodness only
And not also from Religion
Are not accepted
After death
Because there is only
Natural good in their charity
And not spiritual good also;
And it is the spiritual
That conjoins
The Lord to man,
And not the natural
Apart from the spiritual.

T.537

Diabolical Love

Diabolical love
Is the love of self.
It is called love
Although viewed in itself
It is hatred;
For it loves no one
Outside of itself;
Neither does it desire
To be joined with others
In order to benefit them
But only
To benefit itself.

T.45

Successive Churches

There have been
Several churches
On this earth
And in the course of time
They have all been
Consummated
And after their consummation
New churches have arisen
And so on
To the present time.
The consummation
Of the church takes place
When there is
No Divine truth left
Except what has been
Falsified or set aside,
And where there is
No genuine truth
No genuine good is possible
Since every quality of good
Is formed
By means of truths.

T.753

Into Its Order

Every beast of the earth,
Every bird of heaven,
Every fish of the sea,
Every reptile and every worm,
Even to the moth,
Has been created
Into its own order;
Equally so
Every forest tree and fruit tree,
Every shrub and plant;
And still further
Every stone,
Every mineral
Down to every grain of dust
Has been created
Into its order.

T.54

Perpetually

The prolification
Of the truths of Faith
May be compared
To the prolification
Of seeds in a field
Or a garden
Which may be propagated
To myriads of myriads
Perpetually.

T.350

Into Every Part

The spirit of man
Acts into every part
Of the body,
(Even the minutest)
Insomuch that if any part
Is not actuated
By the spirit,
Or the spirit is not
Active in it,
It does not live.

H.453

Like Himself

It is to be observed
That a man after death
Is not natural
But a spiritual man.
Nevertheless
He still appears
In all respects
Like himself,
And so much so
That he knows not
But that he is still
In the natural world
For he has a similar
Body, countenance,
Speech, and senses.

CL.31

Father Approached

When the Lord God
The Savior
Is approached,
God the Father
Is approached also;
Therefore to Philip
Asking Him
To show them the Father
He replied
"He that hath seen Me
Hath seen the Father."

T.538

Raised Up

Since Faith
In its essence is truth
It follows that
According to the abundance
And coherence of truths
It becomes more and more
Perfectly spiritual,
For it is raised up
Into the higher region
Of the mind
From which it sees
Beneath it
Troops of confirmations
Of itself
In the nature of the world.

T.352

More Sensual

Men of learning and erudition
Who have confirmed themselves
Deeply in falsities,
And still more
Those who have
Confirmed themselves
Against the truths of the Word
Are more sensual than others.

T.565

Spiritual Mines

The Word is like a mine
Containing in its depths
Gold and silver
In great abundance
And like a mine which
(At greater and greater depths)
Conceals stones
More and more precious;
These mines are opened
In the measure
Of man's understanding
Of the Word.

T.245

Emanation

Spiritual things
Cannot proceed
From any other source
Than Jehovah God
Who is love itself;
Hence the Sun
Of the Spiritual World
Is pure Love
Proceeding from Jehovah God
Who is in the midst of it.
That Sun is not God
But is an emanation
From God.

S.B.5

One Life

Man has
Both a life of truth
And a life of good;
A life of truth
In his understanding
And a life of good
In his will
And when these are made one
They constitute one life.

T.259

Loves More

Love to the neighbor in man
Ascends
More and more interiorly.
And as it ascends
He loves a community
More than an individual,
And his country
More than a community.

T.413

Came to Save

The Lord
Came into the world
That He might effect
Salvation of the Human Race
Which must.
Otherwise have perished
In eternal death.

HD.293

Interiors Closed

It has been granted me
To speak
With many of the learned
After their departure
From the world;
Those that had in heart
Denied the Divine
(Whatever their professions
Had been)
Had become so stupid
As to have
Little comprehension
Even of any civil truth,
Still less
Of any spiritual truth.
I perceived and also saw
That the interiors of their minds
Were so closed up
As to appear black.

H.354

Part Three

Alpha and Omega

"I am
The Alpha and Omega,
The Beginning and the End,
The First and the Last;
Blessed are they
That do His Commandments
That they may have right
To the Tree of Life
And may enter in
Through the gates
Into the City."
These words signify
That they enjoy
Eternal felicity
Who live according
To the Lord's Commandments
To the end
That they may be
In the Lord
And the Lord in them by love
And in the New Church
By knowledges
Concerning Him.
By "blessed"
Are signified they
Who enjoy the felicity
Of Eternal life.
"That they may have right
To the Tree of Life"
Signifies to the end
That they may be in the Lord
And the Lord in them by love.
By "entering through the gates
Into the City"
Is signified
That they may be
In the Lord's New Church
By knowledges concerning Him.
And by the "city of Jerusalem"
Is signified the New Church
With its Doctrine.
The "Tree of Life"
Denotes the Lord
As to the Divine Love.

R.951

Who Wholly Deny

Liberty and rationality
Cannot be given the those
In the Christian world
Who wholly deny
The Lord's Divinity
And holiness of the Word
And who confirm this denial
To the end of life;
For this is meant by the sin
Against the Holy Spirit
Which is not forgiven
Either in this world
Or in the world to come.

P.98

Only Those

Only those who approach
The very God
Of Heaven and earth
Can enter Heaven
Because Heaven is Heaven
From that only God
And this God
Is the Lord Jesus Christ
Who is the Lord Jehovah —
From Eternity the Creator,
From Time the Redeemer,
And to Eternity
The Regenerator.

T.26

Love Purified

When love has been purified
By wisdom in the understanding
It becomes
Spiritual and celestial,
But when love has been
Defiled in the understanding
It becomes
Sensual and corporeal.

P.15

Life of Charity

A life of piety
Separated
From a life of charity
Does not lead to Heaven,
But a life of charity does;
And a life of charity
Consists in acting
Honestly and justly
In every employment,
In every business,
And in every work
From an interior
Heavenly motive.

H.535

Love to Do Good

To do good which is really such
Man must act
From the love of good,
And thus
For the sake of good.
They who are influenced
By this love
Are unwilling
So much as to hear of merit,
For they love to do good
And have a lively perception
Of satisfaction in doing it.

HD.151

Mutually Unite

Loving what is good
In another
From the good
In oneself
Is genuine love
To the neighbor
For the goods then kiss
And mutually unite
With each other.

T.418

Everywhere Present

The Spiritual Sun
Is everywhere present
By its heat and light.
It is the circle
Most closely surrounding
The Lord,
Emanating
Both from the Divine Love
And from
His Divine Wisdom,
For the Lord
Is in the midst
Of that Sun.

T.365

Cannot Be Compelled

No one can be compelled
To do good
Because nothing forced
Is permanent with man
(It not being his own);
That alone becomes good
Which he does from liberty
And in accordance
With his reason.

HD.271

All Things

All things in the Universe
That are in Divine order
Have relation
To good and truth;
For nothing can exist
In heaven or the world
That does not have relation
To these two.
This is because
Both of these
Good as well as truth
Go forth from God.

T.398

Many Worlds

By means of the Spiritual Sun
The Universe was created
By Jehovah God.
By the Universe we mean
The whole expanse of worlds
Which are as many
As the stars
In the expanse of our heaven.
Creation was effected
By means of that Sun,
Which is pure Love,
Thus by Jehovah God.
This is meant
By these words in John,
"The Word was with God,
And the Word was God,
All things were made by Him,
And without Him,
Nothing was made
Which was made."

SB.5

All Those Taught

All those
Who are taught by the Lord
From the Word
Are taught a few truths
In the world
But many
When they become angels.

P.172

Good to All

All who are in hell
Wish to do evil
To all,
While those
Who are in Heaven
Wish to do good
To all.

P.215

Under Auspices

Since every man
Lives forever after death
And is allotted a place
According to his life
Either in Heaven or in hell.
It follows
That the Human Race
Throughout the whole world
Is under the Lord's auspices.

P.203

Love Shines Forth

In angels
The likeness and image
Of God
Clearly appear
Since love from within
Shines forth in their faces
(And wisdom in their beauty)
And their beauty
Is a form of their love.

DLW.358

Dark and Sad

Compelled worship
Is corporeal, lifeless,
Darkened, and sad —
Corporeal
Because it is of the body
And not of the mind,
Lifeless
Because there is
No life in it,
Darkened
Because there is
No understanding in it,
And sad
Because there is
No enjoyment
Of Heaven in it.

P.137

Holy Spirit

The Holy Spirit
Is the same as the Lord
And is Truth itself
From which man
Has enlightenment.
Jesus said,
"When the Spirit of Truth
Is come,
He will guide you
Into all Truth."

DLW.149

Of Highest Importance

Since love constitutes
The life of man,
And man is to live
To Eternity
Either in Heaven or in hell
In accordance with the life
He acquired in the world,
It is a matter
Of the highest importance
To know how man acquires
Heavenly love
And becomes imbued with it,
So that his life,
Which is to have no end
May be blessed and happy.

E.837

Not Excusable

Those who have made themselves
Atheists by confirmations
In favor of nature
Are not excusable,
Because they might
Have confirmed themselves
In favor of the Divine;
Ignorance
Does not remove falsity.

DLW.350

Becomes New

So far as man
Knows and understands truths
And wills and does them,
So far he becomes
A new man —
That is,
A regenerate man,
And thus becomes
An angel of Heaven
And has a Heavenly
Love and life.

E.837

Distinctly One

In man
Love and wisdom
Appear as two separate things
Yet in themselves
They are distinctly one
Because with man
Wisdom is such
As the love is,
And the love is such
As the wisdom is.

DLW.39

Continuation

Natural death
Is nothing but resurrection
For the reason
That when the body dies
Man rises again
In respect to his spirit,
And thus death is simply
A continuation of life
In the natural world
Into a life
In the Spiritual World.

E.899

Jehovah Descended

The Lord our Savior
Is Jehovah the Father
In Human Form;
For Jehovah descended
And becomes Man
That He might be able
To draw near to man,
And man to Him,
And conjunction
Might thus be effected,
And through that conjunction
Man might have Salvation
And eternal life.

T.370

Merely Natural

He who practices charity
But does not
Acknowledge the Lord
As God of Heaven and earth,
One with the Father
(As He Himself teaches)
Practices merely
Natural charity
In which there is
No eternal life.

T.367

All The Infinites

The heat and light
That go forth
From the Lord as a Sun
Contain in their bosom
All the infinites
That are in the Lord —
The heat
All the infinities of His Love,
And the light
All the infinites
Of His Wisdom.

T.365

Death

So far as a man loves wisdom
Or so far as wisdom
Embosomed in love
Is within him,
So far he is an image of God —
That is,
A receptacle of life
From God;
But on the contrary
So far as he is possessed
By opposite love
(And thence by insanity)
So far as he does not receive
Life from God
But from hell
Which life is called death.

SB.13

Instructed by Angels

Every one is instructed
After death by angels
And those are received
Who sees truths;
But truths are seen
Only by those
Who have not confirmed themselves
In falsities.

T.255

Made True

Falses are made true
By good
And grow soft
When they are applied
And turned to good,
And evil is removed.
Falses of Religion
With those who are in good
Are received by the Lord
As truths.

HD.21

Turn Their Faces

All the angels of Heaven
Turn their faces
To the Lord as a Sun
And all the spirits of hell
Turn their faces
Away from Him.
This makes clear
What the acknowledgment
Of God accomplishes
And what the denial
Of God accomplishes.
And those who deny God
In the world
Deny Him after death.

P.326

Good Works

Works done by man
Are not good
But only those
That are done
By the Lord in man;
But for works to be done
By the Lord
And not by man
Two things are necessary —
First, there must be
An acknowledgement
Of the Lord's Divine
That He is the God
Of Heaven and earth
Even in respect
To his Human
And secondly
It is necessary
That man live by the
Commandments
Of the Decalogue.
These two things
Are necessary
That the works done by man
May be good.

E.934

Charity and Faith

Charity is everything
That pertains to life,
And faith everything
That pertains to doctrine.
Consequently
Charity is willing and doing
What is just and right
In every work.
And faith
Is thinking
Justly and rightly.

H.364

He Loveth Me

They alone love God
Who love the Divine things
That are from Him
In that they do them;
For the Lord says:
"He that hath My Commandments
And doeth them
He it is that loveth Me."

P.326

Bride and Wife

What the New Church
Is to be
Is fully described
In the Apocalypse
Where the end
Of the former church
And the beginning
Of the new
Are treated of.
This New Church
Is described
By the New Jerusalem.
By its magnificence,
And by its being
The future Bride and Wife
Of the Lamb.

T.790

New Jerusalem

By the "New Jerusalem"
Coming down from God
Out of Heaven
A New Church is meant
For the reason that Jerusalem
Was the metropolis
In the land of Canaan
And the Temple and altar
Were there,
And the sacrifices
Were offered there,
Thus the Divine worship
Itself was there,
And also for the reason
That the Lord was in Jerusalem
And taught in its Temple
And afterwards
Glorified His Human there.
This is why "Jerusalem"
Signifies the church.

T.782

Repent

Actual repentance
Is to examine oneself,
To recognize one's sins,
To confess them before God,
And thus to begin
A new life.

T.561

Clearer Light

When man's thought
Is raised above sensual things
He comes into clearer light
And at length
Into Heavenly light,
And then he has perception
Of such things
As flow down from Heaven.

T.565

Heat and Light

Heat from the Sun
Of the Spiritual World
In the midst of which
Is Jehovah God
Is in its essence
Divine Love
And the light from it
Is in its essence
Divine Wisdom.

T.49

Those Love

To love truth and good
For the sake
Of truth and good
Is to will it and do it;
For those love
Who will and do,
While those who do not
Will and do,
Do not love.

H.350

God Cannot

How deluded they are
Who think,
And still more
Who teach
That God can damn any one
Curse any one,
Send any one to hell,
Predestine any soul
To eternal death,
Avenge wrongs,
Be angry or punish.
God cannot even
Turn Himself
Away from man,
Nor look upon him
With a stern countenance.

T.56

Seen As Men

That angels and spirits
Are men
May plainly appear
From those seen
By Abraham, Daniel,
Gideon,
And the Prophets
And especially by John
When he wrote the
Apocalypse
And also by the women
In the Lord's sepulchre,
Yea, from the Lord Himself
As seen by the Disciples
After His Resurrection.

CL.30

Three things

There are three things
By which Faith
Is formed in man;
First by going to the Lord,
Secondly, by learning
Truths from the Word,
And thirdly,
By living according to them.

T.348

Last and First

Sensual things
Ought to occupy
The last place,
Not the first;
And in a wise man
They do occupy the last place
And are subordinate
To things inferior;
But in a foolish man
They occupy the first place
And are predominant.

T.565

God's Descent

The Lord frequently said
That the Father sent Him
And that He was
Sent by the Father
And this He said because
"Being sent into the world"
Means to descend
And come among men
And this was done
By means of the Human
Which He took on
Through the Virgin Mary.

T.92

Actuating Power

The actuating power
Of the natural sun
Is not from itself
But from a living force
Proceeding from the Sun
Of the Spiritual World.
Consequently,
If the living force
Of that Sun were withdrawn
Or taken away
The natural sun would have
No vital power.

DLW.157

Truths Inscribed

Truths ought to be taken
From the Word
Because all truths
That conduce to Salvation
Are in the Word,
And there is efficacy in them
Because they are given
By the Lord
And are therefore inscribed
On the whole angelic Heaven.

T.347

Worship from Love

Whatever is inseminated
In the mind
While in a state of liberty
Remains.
But what is inseminated
By compulsion
Does not remain
Because it is not
From the will
Of the man himself
But from the will
Of him who compels;
Hence it is
That worship from liberty
Is pleasing to the Lord
And that worship
From compulsion
Is not so;
For the former worship
Is from love
But the latter is not.

HD.143

Real Sanctities

External sanctity is found
With the evil
As well as with the good;
And they who place
The whole of Divine worship
In it
Are for the most part
Extremely ignorant;
That is —
They are destitute
Of good and truth,
Which yet form
The real sanctities
Which are to be known,
Believed and loved;
Because they are from God
And God is in them.

HD.125

Unwilling

Those who have
Confirmed themselves
In falsities
Are unwilling to see truths
Or if they see them
They turn themselves away
And either ridicule
Or falsify them.

T.255

Only One Fountain

The Divine Providence
Extends
To the most minute particulars
Of the life of man;
For there is only
One Fountain of Life;
From whom we have our being,
From whom we live,
And from whom we act;
And that Fountain
Is the Lord.

HD.268

Procures Wisdom

He becomes
Prosperous and blessed
Who procures to himself
Wisdom
And keeps his will
Under its obedience
But unprosperous and unhappy
If he puts his understanding
Under obedience
To his will;
The reason is
Because the will
Hereditarily tends to evils,
Even to those
Which are enormous.

SB.14

Cannot Condemn

No man of sound reason
Can condemn wealth,
For it is in the general body
Like the blood in a man,
Nor can he condemn
The honors attached to office
For they are
The hands of the king
And the pillars of society.
Moreover there are
Administrative offices
In Heaven
And honors
Attached to them.

T.403

At Once

In Heaven
Those are called wise
Who are in good,
And those are in good
Who apply Divine truths
At once to life
For as soon as Divine truth
Comes to be of life
It becomes good.

H.348

Sensual Man

He is called a sensual man
Who judges everything
From the bodily senses
And believes nothing
But what he can see
With eyes
And can touch
With his hands
Calling that something real
And rejecting
Everything else.

T.565

Perishable

Charity and faith
Are persishable things
So long as they are
Merely mental
Or unless they are determined
To works
And coexist in them
When possible.

T.376

Everyone's Life

The poor come into Heaven
Not on account of their poverty
But because of their life.
Everyone's life follows him
Whether he be rich or poor;
There is no peculiar mercy
For one
In preference to another.
He that has lived well
Is received
While he that has not
Lived well
Is rejected.

H.364

New Church

The Ancient Church
Followed the Most Ancient,
And after the Ancient Church
The Israelitish or Jewish
Church followed,
And after this the Christian.
It is foretold
In the Apocalypse
That this will be followed
By a New Church
Which is there meant
By the "New Jerusalem"
Coming down out of Heaven.

P.328

In Heart

When a man acts from Religion
He acknowledges in heart
That there is a God,
A Heaven and a hell,
And a life after death,
But when he acts
Merely from regard
To civil and moral laws
He may act in the same way
And yet in heart may deny
That there is a God,
A Heaven and a hell,
And a life after death.

E.902

His Abode

Let no one believe
That the Lord is with those
Who merely worship Him;
He is with those
Who do His commandments
Thus who perform uses;
With such He has His abode.

DLW.335

Even Is Himself

The Word is the Lord
Because it is from the Lord,
For the reason
That the Word is Divine Truth:
And Divine Truth
Goes forth from the Lord
As a Sun;
And what goes forth
Belongs to Him
From whom it goes forth,
And even is Himself;
Consequently,
The Divine Truth
Is the Lord in Heaven.

E.797

The Savior

Saving faith is to believe
That the Lord
Is the Savior of the world
And that He is the God
Of Heaven
And the God of the earth,
And that by His Coming
Into the world
He entered into the power
To save all
Who receive truths from Him
Through the Word
And who live
According to them.

E.808

Spiritual Objects

In the Heavens
Truths are spiritual objects
And they appear more clearly
Before the angels there
Than natural objects do
Before men in the world;
Consequently they know
That faith is nothing else
Than acknowledgment of truth
Because it is seen
To be true.

E.831

All Impiety

In the most general sense
Profanation means
All impiety;
And therefore profaners mean
All the impious,
Who in heart deny God,
The holiness of the Word,
And the spiritual things
Of the church.

P.229

Form of the Spirit

What the form of man's spirit is
I have frequently been shown,
And with some who were
Beautiful and charming
In appearance
The spirit was seen
To be so deformed,
Black, and monstrous
That it might be called
An image of hell,
Not of Heaven;
While in others
Not beautiful in outward form
There was a spirit
Beautifully formed,
Pure and angelic.
Moreover the spirit of man
Appears after death
Such as it has been
In the body
While it lived therein
In the world.

H.99

Unceasingly Desires

The Divine of the Lord
In Heaven is love,
For the reason
That love is receptive
Of all things of Heaven
Such as peace, intelligence,
Wisdom, and happiness.
For love is receptive
Of each and all things
That are in harmony with it;
It longs for them,
Seeks them,
And drinks them in
Spontaneously
For it desires unceasingly
To be enriched and perfected
By them.

H.18

Love Makes Man

No truth ever enters
Into the life of man
Unless the man
Be in good,
For good is of love,
And love
Makes the whole man;
A man therefore
Receives into his life
All truths that agree
With his love.

E.6

Even Perceives

Every one in the Heavens
Knows and believes
And even perceives
That he wills and does
Nothing of good from himself,
But on from the Divine,
Thus from the Lord.

H.8

Best of Angels

In the Heavens there are some
That dwell apart,
House by house as it were,
And family by family.
Although these
Live in this scattered way
They are arranged in order
Like those
Who live in societies.
The wiser in the middle
And the more simple
In the borders.
Such are more directly
Under the Divine auspices
Of the Lord,
And are the best of angels.

H.50

Language of Angels

It is an arcanum
Hitherto unknown
That there is
A universal language
Which is the language
Of all angels and spirits
And which has
Nothing in common
With any language of men
In the world.
Into this language
Everyone comes after death.

T.19

Spirit of Truth

As the Lord
Is truth itself
All that goes forth from Him
Is truth
And this is what is meant
By the Comforter
Who is also called
The Spirit of Truth.

T.139

Like a Sponge

If a man's life
Has been a life
Of the love of evil,
Every truth that
He has acquired in the world
From a teacher,
From preaching,
Or from the Word
Is taken away,
And when truth
Has been taken away
He imbibes such falsity
As agrees with his evil
As a sponge imbibes water.

P.17

Opposite Loves

Loves are manifold,
But two of them,
Heavenly love
And infernal love,
Are like lords and kings.
Heavenly love is love
To the Lord and love
Towards the neighbor;
And infernal love
Is love of self
And of the world.
These two loves
Are opposites
As hell and Heaven.

P.106

Hypocrites Are Such

Hypocrites are such
As have been accustomed
To talk like angels
But interiorly
Have acknowledged
Nature
Alone
And not the Divine
And have therefore denied
What pertains to Heaven
And the church.

H.458

It Is Divine

What is honest and just
Should be done
For the sake
Of honesty and justice
Because the Divine
That goes forth from the Lord
Is in it
And consequently
Regarded in its very essence
It is Divine.

H.472

Two Senses

Inasmuch as Divine truth
Passed down through the Heavens
Even to the world
It became adapted
To angels in Heaven
And also to men in the world.
For this reason
There is in the Word
A spiritual sense
In which the Divine truth
Is seen in clear light
And a natural sense
In which it is seen
Obscurely.

                                            T.85

Kingdom of God

The Kingdom of God
Means both
Heaven and the church
For the church
Is the Kingdom of God
On earth.

                                            T.572

Faith's Sight

Faith's sight
Is like one's seeing
A bright cloud
And in the midst of it
An angel
Who invites the man to him
So that he may be raised
Into Heaven.
Thus does the Lord appear
To those who have faith
In Him.
He draws near to every man
So far as man recognizes
And acknowledges Him.

                                            T.339

Influx

Divine influx
Is into the souls of men
Because the soul
Is the inmost
And highest part of man
And the influx from God
Enters into that
And descends therefrom
Into the things that are below
And vivifies them
In accordance with reception.

                                            T.8

Like Gangrene

The sins
An impenitent man
Holds fast to
May be compared
To various diseases in him
From which he dies
Unless remedies are applied
And the malignities
Thereby removed.
Sins may be compared especially
To the disease gangrene
Which unless healed in time
Spreads and causes
Inevitable death.

                                            T.524

Salvation

Unless evils are removed
By repentance
Man cannot love his neighbor,
Still less God;
Yet on these two Commandments
Hang the law and the prophets —
That is,
The Word,
Consequently Salvation.

                                            T.530

In Mind and Body

The man who looks primarily
To himself and the world
Is an external man,
Because he is natural
Not only in body
But also in mind;
While the man
Who looks primarily
To the things
Of Heaven and the church
Is an internal man
Because he is spiritual
Both in mind and body.

T.420

Mistaken Blessings

Whoever
Rightly considers the subject
May know
That worldly rank and riches
Are not real Divine blessings
Although man
From the pleasure they yield him
Calls them so:
For they pass away
And also seduce many
And turn them away
From Heaven.

HD.270

Implanted

When a Heavenly life's love
Has been implanted
By the Lord
In place
Of an infernal life's love,
Affections for good and truth
Are implanted
In place of the lusts
Of evil and falsity.

P.126

Ordained from Creation

A state of marriage
Is to be preferred
Because it is a state
Ordained from creation
Because it originates
In the marriage
Of good and truth
And because it corresponds
With the marriage
Of the Lord
And the church.

CL.156

Wise Ancients

The ancients
From the wise to the simple.
Thought of God
No otherwise
Than as being a Man
And when at length
They began to worship
A plurality of gods
As at Athens and Rome
They worshipped them all
As men.

DLW.11

Loves Neighbor

The man who does good
Of any kind
For its own sake,
And who acts
Sincerely and justly
For the sake
Of sincerity and justice,
Loves the neighbor
And exercises charity;
For he acts
From the love of good,
Sincerity, and justice.

HD.103

Glorifies Him

By conflicts and temptations
In the world
The Lord
Glorified His Human —
That is,
He made it Divine;
In like manner now
With man individually
(When he is in temptations)
The Lord fights for him,
Conquers the evil spirits
That are infesting him,
And after temptation
Glorifies him —
That is,
Renders him spiritual.

T.599

Wakefulness

An unregenerate man
Is like one dreaming
And a regenerate man
Like one awake
And in the Word
Natural life
Is likened to sleep
And spiritual life
To a state of wakefulness

T.606

In Every Society

A copy of the Word
Written by angels
Who are inspired by the Lord
Is kept
In every larger Society
In its sacred repository
That it may not be changed
Elsewhere
In the least point.

T.241

Sense of Letter

The Word
Without the sense
Of its letter
Would be like a palace
Without a foundation
And thus
Like a palace in the air
Instead of on the earth
Which would be
Only the shadow of a palace
That would vanish away.

T.213

Theater of Uses

The Universe
Was created by God
To give existence to uses
And for this reason
The Universe may be called
A theatre of uses

T.67

Counter

Since man's
Internal and external
Can run
Counter to each other,
And since the body
Is cast aside
While the spirit remains,
A dark spirit
May evidently dwell
Behind a bright face
And a fiery one
Behind a bland mouth.
Therefore my friend
Form your opinion
Of a man
Not from his mouth
But from his heart.

T.590

Shining Forms

In the Spiritual Heaven
There are magnificent palaces
In which all things within
Shine with precious stones
And decorations
In such forms
As cannot be equalled
By any painting in the world
Nor expressed in words.
From that Heaven
Many arts in the world
Derive their laws and harmonies
From which come
Their forms of beauty.

E.831

Surpassing Joy

When certain spirits
Wished to know
What Heavenly joy is
They were allowed to feel it
To such a degree
That they could no longer
Bear it.

H.410

What He Thinks

So long as a man
Is living in the world
He is wholly ignorant
Of what he thinks
In the spiritual mind;
He knows only what he thinks
From that mind
In the natural;
But after death
The state is changed,
And he then thinks
From the spiritual mind
And not from the natural.

E.790

Endowed

So far as a man shuns evils
And turns away from them
Because they are sins,
And thinks about
Heaven, Salvation,
And eternal life,
So far he is adopted
By the Lord
And conjoined to Heaven,
And so far he is endowed
With spiritual affection.

E.837

Not Acknowledged

The Lord
Is not acknowledged
When His Divine in His Human
Is not acknowledged,
For the reason that the Lord
Is not then regarded
As God
But only as a man;
And a man
Is not able to save.

E.807

Wishes to Enter

When a man shuns
And turns away from evils,
All things
That he thinks:
Wills, and does
Are good
Because they are
From the Lord;
For the Lord
Is continually present,
Knocks at the door,
Is urgent,
And wishes to enter.

E.798

To Rise Again

"Every one that liveth
And believeth in Me
Shall never die"
Signifies
That he who has been reformed
Shall not die spiritually, —
That is, be damned,
But shall rise again
Into eternal life.
This makes clear
That "to die"
Does not mean to die
But to rise again
To life.

E.899

Holiest Solemnity

The Holy Supper
Was instituted by the Lord
To be a means
Whereby the church
May have conjunction
With Heaven
And thus with the Lord;
It is therefore
The holiest solemnity
Of Divine worship.

HD.210

Only by Means

Divine Love
Wills to save all
But it can save only
By means of Divine Wisdom;
To Divine Wisdom
Belong all the laws
Through which
Salvation is effected;
And these laws
Love cannot transcend.

DLW.37

Lord God

It is never granted
To any man of the church
To approach God the Father
Immediately,
And to pray to Him
For the Son's sake;
For it is the Lord
Who must be approached
And prayed to,
Since no one comes to the Father
Except by the Lord
And in the Lord;
And the Lord
Equally as the Father
Is God.

E.805

Full of Delights

That viewed in itself
It is nothing else
Than blessedness and delight;
Thus whether you say
Heaven or Heavenly joy
It is the same thing.

H.397

Deathbed Fallacy

That man can receive faith
And be saved
At the hour of death
Whatever his life
May have been
Is a fallacy,
Since a man's life
Continues the same,
And he is judged
According to his deeds
And works.

E.781

Formed for Heaven

I have spoken
With some after death who
While they lived in the world
Renounced the world
And gave themselves up
To an almost solitary life
In order that by abstraction
Of the thoughts
From worldly things
They might have opportunity
For pious meditations
Believing
That thus they might enter
The way to Heaven.
But these in the Other life
Are of a sad disposition;
They despise others
Who are not like themselves
They are indignant
That they do not have
A happier lot than others
Believing they have merited it.
They have no interest
In others
And turn away
From the duties of charity
By which there is conjunction
With Heaven.
They desire Heaven
More than others
But when they are taken up
Among angels
They induce anxieties
And are sent away
And when sent away
They betake themselves
To desert places
Where they lead a life
Like that
Which they lived
In the world.
Man can be formed for Heaven
Only by means of the world.

H.360

Such Love

Divine Love is such
That it wills its own
To be another's,
Thus to be the man's
Or the angel's.
Such is all spiritual love
And pre-eminently
The Divine Love.

P.43

Affections

Every one has good affections
So far as he has shunned
Evils as sins,
And every one has
Evil affections
So far as he has not
So shunned them.

P.61

God's Divine Natural

The Glorification of the Lord
Was the Glorification
Of His Human
Which He assumed in the world,
And the Lord's Glorified Human
Is the Divine Natural.
The truth of this is evident
From the fact that the Lord rose
From the tomb
With the whole of the body
That He had in the world
Leaving nothing in the tomb
And therefore took with Him
From the tomb
The Natural Human itself
From the firsts to the lasts.
By means of His Glorification
His natural body
Was made Divine.

T.109

City of Truth

That "Jerusalem" means
A church
About to be established
By the Lord
And not the Jerusalem
Inhabited by the Jews
Is evident
From the particulars
Of its description
As that Jehovah God
Was to create
A new Heaven and earth
And after that
Jerusalem
And that she should be
A crown of glory
And a royal diadem;
That she should be called
Holiness,
A city of Truth
The throne of Jehovah,
A quiet habitation,
A tabernacle
That should not
Be taken down.

T.782

The Church

The Lord's Heaven
In the natural world
Is called the church,
And an angel of that Heaven
Is a man of the church
Who is conjoined
With the Lord
And who becomes an angel
Of the Spiritual Heaven
After he leaves
This world.

P.30

Like Fire

Lusts with their enjoyments
May be likened to fire.
The more a fire is fed
The more it burns;
And the freer the course
Given to it
The more it spreads.
In the Word
The lusts of evil
Are likened to fire,
And their evils
To its burning.

P.112

Continually

Such evils as a man
Believes to be allowable
Even though
He does not do them
Are appropriated to him
Since whatever is made
Allowable in the thought
Comes from the will
And there is then consent,
And he does them
Continually
In his spirit.

P.81

Receptacle

The Divine order is
That man should set himself
In order
For the reception of God
And prepare himself
To be a receptacle and abode
Into which God may enter.

T.105

Can Never Be

It was never possible
(Nor can it ever be)
That any angel of Heaven
Should descend,
Or any spirit of hell
Ascend
And speak with any man
Except with those
Who have the
Interiors of the mind
Or spirit
Opened by the Lord.

CL.39

The Spiritual Dispels

The internal of every good
And of every truth
Is spiritual,
And the spiritual
Dispels falsities and evils
While the natural by itself
Favors them,
And favoring falsities and evils
Is not in accord with good.

P.14

Beauty of Faith

Faith in its essence
Is truth giving light;
Consequently,
The beauty and comeliness
Of Faith
Caused by that glow
Are multiplied
And may be compared
To the precious stones
Of various colors
In the breastplate of Aaron
Which together were called
The Urim and Thummim.

T.353

Rare

I am aware
That few will acknowledge
That all joys and delights
From first to last
Are collected
Into conjugial love
Because love truly conjugial
Into which they are collected
Is at this day
So rare
That its quality
Is not known
And scarcely its existence.

CL.69

Reciprocal Love

In Heavenly marriages
There is no predominance;
For the will of the wife
Is also the husband's will
And the understanding
Of the husband is also
The wife's understanding
Since the love of each
Is to will and think
Like the other,
That is,
Mutually and reciprocally.
Thus they are conjoined
Into one.

H.369

Into the Heavens

I have been taken by the Lord
Into the Heavens
And to the earths in the Universe
And it was my spirit
That so journeyed
While my body remained
In the same place.

H.192

Not Encompassed

The spirit of man
After the dissolution of the body
Appears in the Spiritual World
In a human form,
In every respect
As in the natural world.
He enjoys
The faculty of sight,
Of hearing,
Of speaking,
And of feeling
As he did in the world;
And he is endowed
With every faculty
Of thought,
Of will,
And of action
As when he was in the world;
In a word,
He is a man in all respects
Even to the most
Minute particular,
Except that he is not encompassed
With the gross body
Which he had in the world.

HD.225

Cannot Shine

Those who love truths
Either with glory in the world
Or glory in Heaven
As an end
Cannot shine in Heaven
Since they are
Delighted and affected
By the light of the world
And not with the
Very light of Heaven;
And the light of the world
Without the light of Heaven
Is in Heaven
Mere thick darkness.

H.347

Daily Repentance

He who lives in practice
Of charity and faith
Performs the work
Of repentance daily;
He reflects on the evils
That adhere to him,
Acknowledges them,
Guards against them,
And supplicates the Lord
For aid to resist them.

HD.163

Eternal Reward

The delight which is inherent
In the love of doing good
Without any view to reward
Is itself
An eternal reward;
For Heaven
An eternal happiness
Are inseminated
Into that good
By the Lord.

HD.156

Afterwards to Eternity

The life of Heaven
Can be implanted in no one
Unless he abstains from evil,
For evil obstructs.
So far therefore
As man abstains from evil
He is led by the Lord
Out of pure mercy
(By His Divine means)
And this from infancy
To the end of his life
In the world
And afterwards
To Eternity.

H.522

Opens Heaven

The style of the Word is such
That there is a holiness
In every sentence
And in every word
And even in some places
In the very letters
And thereby the Word
Conjoins men with the Lord
And opens Heaven.

T.191

In Highest Degree

The Lord's Kingdom
Is the neighbor
That is to be loved
In the highest degree
Because the Lord's Kingdom
Means the church
Throughout the world
Which is called
The communion of saints;
Also Heaven is meant by it.

T.416

New Light

It has been granted to me
To talk with angels
As man with man,
Also to see the things
That are in the Heavens
And that are in the hells
And for the reason
That the end
Of the present church
Has come
And the beginning
Of a new one
Which will be
The New Jerusalem
Is at hand.

E.1183

Divine Source

Jehovah God
Is Being in Itself
Because He is the I AM,
The Only, and the First
From Eternity to Eternity,
The Source of everything
That is,
Without Whom
It could not be.
In this way
And not otherwise
He is
The Beginning and the End,
The Alpha and Omega,
The First and the Last.

T.21

New Life

Man's regeneration
Is described in Ezekiel
By the "dry bones"
Which were clothed with sinews;
Then with flesh and skin
And at last
Had spirit breathed into them
Whereby they lived again.

T.594

Like Fruits

As the truths of faith
Not only illuminate charity
But also
Determine its quality,
It follows that charity
Without the truths of faith
Is like fruit without juice,
Like a dried-up fig,
Or like a grape
After the wine
Has been pressed out.

T.377

Peaceful Presence

The presence of the Lord
Is unceasing
In all who are in Heaven
And in the church;
And it is a presence
That is peaceful, tranquil,
Preserving, and sustaining,
By which all things
In the Heavens
And on the earth
Are held constantly
In their order
And connection.

E.850

To Love Others

It is essential of love
Not to love self
But to love others
And to be conjoined
With others by love.
The essence of all love
Consists in conjunction;
This is its life.

DLW.47

From the World

From the world
A man knows nothing
About Heaven and hell,
Or a life after death,
Or even about God;
His natural light
Teaches nothing
Except what has entered
Through the eyes,
Thus nothing except
What relates
To the world and to self,
And from these is his life.

E.820

Religion

What is Religion
Except that man may so live
That he may come into Heaven
And that he may know
How to live?
To know this
Is called doctrine;
And to believe it
And live according to it
Is called Religion.

E.805

Life Itself

Because the Lord
Is Uncreate and Infinite
He is Being itself
Which is called
"Jehovah"
And Life itself.

DLW.4

Man Supposes

Man supposes
That even if he lives wickedly
He can still have faith
At least to believe
That there is a God,
That the Lord
Is the Savior of the world,
That there is
Heaven and a hell.
And that the Word is holy.
But I can assert
That if he does not shun evils
Because they are sins,
And also look to the Lord,
He does not at all
Believe these things,
Since they are not
Of his life and love.

E.839

From Reception

Heaven is not Heaven
From anything
That strictly belongs
To the angels
But from the reception
By angels
Of the Divine
Love and Wisdom
From the Lord.

P.163

In God We Live

In the created Universe
Nothing lives except God-Man
(That is, the Lord)
Neither is anything moved
Except by life from Him,
Nor has any being
Except through the sun
From Him;
So that it is a truth
That in God we live,
And move,
And have our being.

DLW.301

Wherever Man Is

The Spiritual World
Is wherever man is
And in no wise
Away from him.
In a word,
Every man
As regards the interiors
Of his mind
Is in that world,
In the midst
Of spirits and angels,
And he thinks from its light
And loves from its heat.

DLW.92

No Favor

A man may be compelled
To speak
In favor of Religion
And to do
What it inculcates,
But he cannot be compelled
To favor it in his thought
From any belief in it,
Or to favor it in his will
From any love for it.

P.129

Appearance

So long as man remains
In this world
No perception by sensation
Can be given him
That he lives
From the Lord alone
Because the appearance
That he lives from himself
Is never taken away.

P.156

Loves Good

Anyone can comprehend
Intellectually
And see rationally
That so far as he flees from
(And turns away from)
Theft and cheating
So far as he loves sincerity,
Rectitude, and justice;
So far as he flees from
(And turns away from)
Revenge and hatred,
So far as he loves the neighbor;
And so far as he flees
And turns away from adulteries
So far he loves chastity.

DLW.419

Mere Idol

It is known
That the doctrines
Of the churches
In the Christian world
Teach that God is One.
This they teach
Because all their doctrines
Are from the Word
And so far as one God
Is acknowledged
Both with their lips
And heart
These doctrines
Are consistent.
To those who confess
One God
With the lips only
But in heart accept three
(As is true of many
At this day)
God is nothing but a word
On the lips,
And all their theology
Is a mere idol
Enclosed in a golden shrine
The key to which
The priests alone hold
And when such read the Word
They perceive no light
Not even that God is One.

T.7

Love First Degree

The reason
Why many in the world
Are not prepared for Heaven
Is that they love
The first degree of their life
Which is called the natural
And are not willing
To withdraw from it
And become spritual.

P.324

Prepared

Every one
Who permits himself
To be led to Heaven
Is prepared
For his own place
In Heaven.

P.67

In Both Worlds

Man was so created by God
That in respect to his internal
He might be
In the spiritual world
And in respect to his external
In the natural world.
Consequently
He was created
A native of both worlds
In order that the spiritual
Which belongs to Heaven
Might be implanted
In the natural
Which belongs to the world.

T.14

Idea of God

A right idea of God
Is like the sanctuary and altar
In a temple
Or like a crown upon the head
And the sceptre in hand
Of a king on his throne,
For upon a right idea of God
The whole body of theology hangs
Like a chain on its first link;
And (if you will believe it)
Everyone is allotted
His place in the Heavens
In accordance
With this idea of God.

T.163

Angelic Heaven

The Lord's Coming
Is for the purpose
Of forming a new Heaven
Of those who have
Believed in Him
And for the purpose
Of establishing a New Church
Of those who shall
Hereafter believe in Him.
The very end
For which the Universe
Was created
Was no other
Than the formation from men
Of an Angelic Heaven.

T.773

Prevents Appearing

If anyone shuns evil
For any reason whatever
Except that they are sins
He does not shun them
But only prevents
Their appearing
Before the world.

P.118

Divine Order

There is an order from which
And according to which
The whole Universe
And all things in it
Was created,
And because all creation
Was effected
From that order
And according to it
God is called
Order itself.

T.500

Communion of Saints

He who in belief
Acknowledges
(And in heart worships)
One God
Is in the communion
Of saints on earth
And in the communion
Of the angels in Heaven
Because such are
In the one God
And the one God
Is in them.

T.15

Not Even from Angels

That the Lord
Manifested Himself
Before me His servant
And sent me to this office;
That He afterwards
Opened the eyes of my spirit
And thus introduced me
Into the Spiritual World
And granted me to see
The Heavens and the hells
And to talk
With angels and spirits
And this now continuously
For several years
I affirm in truth;
As also
That from the first day
Of that call
I have not received
Anything whatever
Pertaining to the Doctrines
Of the New Church
From any angel
But from the Lord alone
While I have read
The Word.

T.779

Conjunction

By means of the sense
Of the letter of the Word
There is conjunction
With the Lord
And affiliation
With the angels.
This conjunction
Is effected
By means of the sense
Of the letter
Because the Word
In that sense
Is in its fullness,
In its holiness,
And in its power.

T.234

Brings the Angelic

No one becomes an angel,
That is —
No one comes into Heaven
Unless he carries with him
From the world
What is angelic.

P.60

Angels Confess

Since love and wisdom
Are the Lord's
And are the Lord in Heaven,
And love and wisdom
Constitute
The life of angels,
It is clear that their life
Is the Lord's life
And in the fact is the Lord.
The angels themselves
Confess
That they live
From the Lord.

P.28

More Than Self

In the Heavens
There is joy
In doing good to another
But no joy
In doing good to self
Unless with a view
To its becoming another's
And thus for another's sake,
This is loving the neighbor
More than ones self.

H.406

One Coherent Work

The Universe
Is a coherent work
From first things to last
Because it is a work
That includes
Ends, causes, and effects
In an indissoluble
Connection.
The Universe consists
Of perpetual uses
Brought forth by Wisdom
But initiated by Love.

T.47

Blessedness

As God is Love itself
So is He blessedness itself
For all love
Breathes forth delights
From itself;
And the Divine Love
Breathes forth blessedness,
Happiness, and felicity
To Eternity.
Thus God from Himself
Renders the angels blessed
And men after death.

T.43

Additional Free-Verse Poems from Swedenborg's *Arcana Coelestia*

Only Few Understand
Last Judgment Today

Few at this day know
What is meant
By the Last Judgment.
It is generally supposed
That it is to be accomplished
With the destruction
Of the world;
And it is hence conjectured
That this terrestial globe
Is to perish by fire
Together with all things
That exist in the visible world
And that then
The dead shall rise again
And shall undergo
Their Judgment
When the wicked
Are to be cast into hell
And the good to ascend
Into Heaven.
Those conjectures
Are grounded
In the prophetical parts
Of the Word,
Where mention is made
Of a new Heaven
And a new earth,
And also of the
New Jerusalem —
Mankind not being aware
That the prophetical parts
Of the Word in their
Internal sense have a totally
Different signification
From what appears
In the literal sense;
And that by heaven or the sky
Is not meant
Heaven or the sky
Nor by earth the earth
But the church of the Lord
In general
And with every individual
In particular.

A.2117

Several Last Judgments
Since Earliest Times

By the Last Judgment
Is meant the last time
Of the church;
And also
The last time
Of every one's life;
To speak of it first
As denoting
The last time of the church —
It was the Last Judgment
Of the Most Ancient church
(Or that before the Flood)
When their posterity perished
Whose destruction is described
By the Flood.
It was the Last Judgment
Of the ancient church
(Or that after the Flood)
When almost all
Who belonged to that church
Became idolaters
And were dispersed.
It was the Last Judgment
Of the representative church
Which succeeded among
The posterity of Jacob
When the Ten Tribes
Were carried away captive
And dispersed
Among the nations
And afterwards when the Jews
(After the Lord's Coming)
Were driven
Out of the Land of Canaan
And scattered over the face
Of the whole earth.
The Last Judgment
Of the present church
Which is called
The Christian church
Is what is meant
In the Revelation of John
By the New Heaven
And the new earth.

A.2118

Talked with Jehovah

The Lord had the inmost
And most perfect
Perception of all.
This perception
(As has been stated)
Was a sensation
And perceptive knowledge
Of all things
Which were doing in Heaven
And was
A continual communication
An internal conversation
With Jehovah,
Which none ever had
But the Lord alone.

A.1791

Were Once Men

Devils in the other world
Were once men who
(During their sojurn here)
Lived in hatred,
Revenge, and adultery,
Many of whom
Were then held in superior
Respect and esteem.

A.968

Sent by the Lord

Sometimes infants
Who are in the Other Life
Are sent by the Lord
To infants on earth
Although the infant
On earth
Is altogether
Ignorant thereof;
They have
Most especial delight
In such association.

A.2295

His Flesh and Blood

When men perceive the Word
According to the letter
The angels perceive it
According to the
Internal sense
Thus,
Instead of the flesh
Of the Lord
They perceive
The Divine Good
And instead of His blood
The Divine Truth,
Each from the Lord.
Hence what is holy
Flows in
Through the Word.

A.10,033

Soon Return

Cetain souls
Fresh arrived from the world
Who desire to see
The glory of the Lord
Before they are in such state
As to be capable
Of beholding it
Are cast
(As to their exterior senses)
And inferior faculties)
Into a kind of sweet sleep,
And then their interior
Senses and faculties
Are raised into
An extraordinary degree
Of wakefulness,
And thus they are let
Into the glory of Heaven;
But as soon as wakefulness
Is restored to the exterior
Senses and faculties
They return
To their former state.

A.1982

On the Altar

Everyone may see
That by meat offering
Which was bread
And by a libation
Which was wine
Is not meant merely
Bread and wine
But something
Of the church and Heaven,
Thus things spiritual
And celestial
Which are of Heaven
And of the church,
Otherwise to what purpose
Could bread and wine
Be put upon the fire
Of the altar?

A.10,137

Land of Canaan

The land of Canaan
In the supreme sense
Signifies the Lord;
In the respective sense
Heaven and the church;
And in the singular sense
A man of the church.

A.4447

Heaven's Societies

Mankind in Most Ancient times
Lived distinguished
Into nations, families
And houses,
In order
That the church on earth
Might represent
The Kingdom of the Lord
Where all are disposed
Into societies.

A.1259

Lord's Two States

In proportion as the Lord
Was in the humanity
Which He received
Hereditarily
From the mother
He appeared distinct
From Jehovah,
And adored Jehovah as being
Different from Himself,
But in proportion
As He put off this humanity
The Lord was not
Distinct from Jehovah
But One with Him.
The former state was the Lord's
State of Humiliation,
But the latter
Was the Lord's state
Of Glorification.

A.1999

Carries Life

They who believe
That man can be
Immediately introduced
Into Heaven,
And that this is
Of the mere mercy
Of the Lord
Are much deceived;
If this were possible
All (as many as are in hell)
Would be elevated
Into Heaven,
For the Lord's mercy
Extends to all;
But it is
According to order
That every one
Carries along with him
His life which he had
Lived in the world.

A.7186

Essential Doctrine

The Lord
Is essential Doctrine itself;
Hence it is
That the Lord
Is called the Word
Because the Word
Is Doctrine.

A.3364

On Their Hearts

In the Most Ancient time
When the church was celestial
The written Word was not;
For the men of that church
Had the Word inscribed
On their hearts
Inasmuch as the Lord
Taught them immediately
Through Heaven
What was good
And thereby
What was true.

A.3424

Is Called Heaven

By the Kingdom of God
In its universal sense
Is meant
The universal Heaven;
In a sense
Less universal
The Lord's true church;
And in a particular sense
Every individual
Having a true faith
Or who is regenerated
By the life of faith;
Wherefore such a person
Is called a heaven
Because Heaven is in him.

A.29

Retain the Life

They who have lived
In the thought and practice
Of hatred, revenge,
Cruelty, and adultery,
And thus not in any charity,
Retain after death
The life which they have
Thereby contracted
Including all things
Belonging to such a life,
Even to the
Minutest particulars,
Which successively return.

A.2116

As if No Existence

With the regenerate
The internal man
Has the dominion,
The external being
Obedient and submissive;
But with the unregenerate
The external man rules,
The internal being quiescent
As if it had
No existence.

A.977

Divine Mercy

The Divine Mercy
Is actually the Divine Love
Towards those
Who are in miseries —
That is,
Towards those
Who are in temptations,
For these are in miseries,
And are primarily meant
By the miserable
In the Word.

A.5042

Conscience

With the regenerate man
There is a conscience
Of what is good and true,
And he does good
And thinks truth
From conscience;
The good which he does
Being the good of charity
And the truth
Which he thinks
The truth of faith.
The unregenerate man
Has no conscience.

A.977

They Remember the Sun

It is noted
That the sun of this world
Does not appear to any spirit
Nor anything of light
Thence derived;
For the light of this sun
Is to spirits
As gross darkness
And only remains
In their perception
From having seen it
While they were
In the world.

A.7171

Heaven Itself

When the Lord is present
In His own Divine
In the Heavens
And in the church
He is likewise
The All-in-All there.
Hence,
He is Heaven itself.

A.10,157

When Man Rises

A man rises again
Immediately after death
And then appears to himself
In a body altogether such
As he had in the world,
With a similar face, arms,
Members, hands, feet,
Breast, loins, etc.
Yea, also
When he sees
And touches himself,
He says that he is a man
As he was in the world.

A.5078

The Sower

The Lord
Is He who sows;
The seed is His Word;
And the ground is man, —
As He Himself
Has deigned to declare.

A.29

Exercises Charity

Charity towards the neighbor
Extends itself much wider
Than to the poor and indigent;
Charity towards the neighbor
Consists in doing
What is right
And what is due
In every office.
If a judge does
What is just
For the sake of
What is just,
He exercises charity
Towards his neighbor.

A.8121

Makes Heaven

The Divine of the Lord
Makes the Heavens,
And Heaven
Is with every one
According to his reception
Of love and faith
From the Lord.

A.10,716

An Eternal Truth

It is an eternal truth
That unless the Lord
Had come into the world
And by temptations
Admitted into Himself
Had subdued and overcome
The hells
The Human Race
Must have perished.
And that otherwise
None could have been saved
Who have lived on this earth
From the time
Of the Most Ancient church.

A.1676

Originates in Heaven

No one can know
What love truly conjugial is
And what is the quality
Of its delight
Unless he be
In the good of love
(In the truths of faith)
From the Lord
Since love truly conjugial
Is from Heaven,
And originates
In the marriage
Of good and truth there

A.10,171

Will Be Seen

Many persons say
That they would believe
If any one
Should they come to them
From the Other Life;
It will not therefore
Be seen
Whether they will
Be persuaded of the truth
After having
Hardened their hearts
Against it.

A.1885

Would Fall

Spiritual temptations
Are at this day little known
Not being permitted
In the manner
They formerly were
Because man is not
In the truths of faith
And thus
Would fall under them.

A.762

Principled in Love

The angels
By reason
Of their being principled
In love to the Lord
And in mutual love
Are also principled
In all truth,
And thus in all
Wisdom and intelligence
Not only in respecting things
Spiritual and celestial
But also respecting things
Rational and natural.

A.2572

All Conduce

The Divine Providence
Differs from all other
Leading and control in this,
That Providence
Continually respects
What is Eternal,
And continually
Leads to salvation,
And this by various states —
Sometimes glad ones
Sometimes sorrowful ones
Which man
Is utterly incapable
Of comprehending;
Nevertheless
They all conduce
To his life in Eternity.

A.8560

Dense Clouds

There are with man
Clouds so large and dense
That were he aware of them
He would wonder
How rays of light
From the Lord
Could ever pass through them
So that he could be
Regenerated.

A.1043

The Lord Protects

The Lord by His angels
Protects man
And restrains the evil spirits
From transgressing their limits
And inundating him
With a more powerful influence
Than he is capable
Of sustaining.

A.741

Greatest Temptations

That the Lord
Underwent and endured
Most grevious temptations
(More grevious
Than all in the Universe
Were ever exposed to)
Is not so fully known
From the Word
Where it is only mentioned
That He was in the wilderness
Forty days
And was tempted
Of the Devil.

A.1663

Life of Love

True love
Is love towards the Lord,
And true life
Is the life of Love
From Him,
And true joy
Is the joy of that life.

A.33

Against the Love

In all temptation
Assault is made
Against the love
In which man is principled,
And the degree
Of the temptation
Is according to the degree
Of the love;
If no assault is made
Upon the love
There is no temptation.
To destroy anyone's love
Is to destroy
His very life.

A.1690

Why the Lord Came

The Lord
Came into the world
That He might
Subdue the hells
And reduce all things
Into order
Even in the Heavens, —
Which was effected
By temptations
Admitted into Himself;
And the passion
Of the Cross
Was the ultimate
Of His temptations
By which He fully
Conquered the hells
And arranged the Heavens
Into order,
And at the same time
Glorified His Human;
And unless he had done so
No man could have been
Saved.

A.10,026

Avert and Defend

The Lord never
Commenced the combat
With any hell
But the hells assaulted Him.
It is the same
With every man
Who is under temptation
Or in combat
With evil spirits;
The attendant angels
Never make the assault,
But this is always done
By the evil
Or infernal spirits
Whilst the angels
Only avert and defend.

A.1683

Does Not Appear

It is to be noted
That the sun of this world
Does not appear
To any spirit,
Nor anything of light
Thence derived;
For the light of this sun
Is to spirits
As gross darkness,
And only remains
In their perception
From having seen it
While they were
In this world.

A.7171

Nation Against Nation

By nation
Being stirred up
Against nation
And kingdom
Against kingdom
Is signified
That evil would combat
Against evil
And what is false
With what is false.

A.3353

Must Worship Lord

They who are within the church
And talk of acknowledging
No other God but the
Creator of the Universe
Do not in fact
Acknowledge any God,
Whatsoever they may
Profess or suppose;
Still less do they
Acknowledge the Lord.

A.2156

Become No Truths

If they
Who are principled in evil
Were to be instructed
A thousand ways,
And this instruction
Was of the most
Perfect kind,
Still the truths of faith
With them
Would enter no further
Than into the memory
And would never penetrate
Into the affections
Of the heart.
Wherefore also
The truths of their memory
Are dissipated
And become no truths
In the Other Life.

A.2590

Communion in Heaven

In the Heavens
There is communion
Of all goods;
The peace, intelligence,
Wisdom, and happiness
Of all
Are communicated
To every one there,
And those of every one
Are communicated
To all;
Nevertheless, to each
According to the reception
Of love and faith
From the Lord.
Hence, it is evident
How great
Peace, intelligence,
Wisdom, and happiness
Are in Heaven.

A.10,723

Truth the Medium

To the intent that man
May have Heavenly good
Which he may love
Above himself and the world
It is necessary
That he learn
Truths from the Word
Or from the doctrine
Of the church
Which is from the Word.
Before he knows those truths
He cannot love them
For no affection is given
Of what is unknown,
Hence it is
That truth is the medium
By which man has good.

A.10,661

Celestial Sense

In the inmost Heaven
All things of the Word
Are applied
To the Divine Human
Of the Lord,
For the angels there think
Immediately from the Lord
And perceive the Word
In its inmost sense,
Which is
The celestial sense.

A.10.265

No Forced Salvation

It is impossible
To force men
To salvation,
For if this could be done
All men in the world
Would be saved.

A.8700

Genuine Charity

It is believed that charity
Towards the neighbor
Consists in
Giving to the poor.
In relieving the indigent,
And in doing good to every one;
Nevertheless genuine charity
Consists in acting prudently,
And for the sake of an end
To promote good.

A.8120

Still Have Doubts

Some profess to believe
They shall rise again
But not till the day
Of the Last Judgment;
And the notion
They have conceived
Of that day is that then
All things appertaining
To the visible world
Are to be destroyed;
As however that day
Has been expected in vain
For so many Ages
They still have doubts
As to any resurrection
Ever taking place.

A.1885

Can Meet with All

Angels and spirits
Can meet with all
Whom they have known
Or heard of
And can see them present
And converse with them
Whenever the Lord
Permits.

A.5229

Soul of Heaven

Everything
Celestial and spiritual
(Or all goodness and truth)
Is from the Lord alone
By virtue of which the Lord
Is the All-in-All in Heaven
And this so absolutely
That whatsoever has not
An apperception
Of goodness and truth
As coming from the Lord
Is no longer in Heaven.
This is the sphere
Which prevails
Throughout all Heaven;
This also
Is the soul of Heaven;
And this is the life
Which flows into all
Who are principled
In goodness.

A.1614

No Other Father

Throughout all Heaven
They know no other Father
Than the Lord
Because He and the Father
Are One,
As He Himself said:
"I am the Way,
The Truth,
And the Life.
Philip saith:
Lord, show us the Father.
Jesus saith unto him:
Have I been
So long time with you
And yet
Hast thou not known Me?
He that hath seen Me
Hath seen the Father."

A.15

Refulgent Brightness

All visible colors
In the Other Life
Represent what is
Celestial and spiritual;
The colors originating
In a flame-like brightness
Representing the things
Appertaining to love
And the affection
Of goodness,
And those originating
In a white brightness
The things appertaining
To faith
And the affection of truth.
All colors in the Other Life
Are from these origins,
And therefore they are
Of such refulgent brightness
That no colors in this world
Are to be compared
With them.
There are also colors
Which were never seen
Here on earth.

A.1624

Completely Adapted

Things that are in Heaven
Are completely adapted
To the sense.
Of spirits and angels;
Whilst the things that are
In the light of the solar world
Are utterly invisible to them.
Buildings of stone and wood
Are adapted to the senses
Of men in the body.
Spiritual things correspond
With those that are spiritual
And corporeal things
With those that are corporeal.

A.1628

Before God

To confess sins
Is to know evils,
To see them in himself,
To make himself guilty,
And to condemn himself
On account of them;
When this is done
Before God
It constitutes
The confession of sins.

A.8387

Garden of Eden

The Most Ancient Church
Which was called
Man or Adam
Was in the Land of Canaan;
Consequently,
The Garden of Eden
Was there,
By which was signified
The intelligence and wisdom
Of the men of that church.

A.4447

Compared to Marriage

The marriage
Of good and truth
In Heaven
Is from the Lord,
Wherefore,
The Lord in the Word
Is called
The Bridegroom and Husband,
And Heaven and the church
Is called
The Bride and Wife;
On this account also
Heaven is compared
To a marriage.

A.10,168

Man's Internal

The internal of man
Is that principle
By virtue of which
Man is man
And by which
He is distinguished
From brute animals.
By this internal
He lives after death
And to Eternity
And by which
He is capable of being
Elevated by the Lord
Amongst angels.
It is the very first form
By virtue of which
He becomes and is
A man.

A.1999

How Man Is Saved

Immediate mercy,
Namely,
That which would extend
To every one
From the good pleasure
Alone of God
Is contrary
To the Divine order,
And what is contrary
To Divine order
Is contrary to God,
For order is from God.
His Divine
In Heaven is Order.
For any one to receive
Order in himself
Is to be saved,
Which is effected solely
By living
According to the precepts
Of the Lord.

A.10,659

Light from the Lord

The light in Heaven is such
As to exceed
The noonday light of this world
In a degree surpassing
All belief.
The Heavenly inhabitants
However,
Receive no light
From this world
Because they are
Above or within
The sphere of that light,
But they receive light
From the Lord
Who to them is a sun.

A.1521

Appropriates Evils

A man who is not principled
In faith towards the Lord
Cannot be enlightened
But supposes
That evil is from himself
And thus appropriates it
To himself
And becomes
Like the evil spirits
Who attend him.

A.761

Abhor Merit

To do good
Which is good
Must be
From the love of good
Thus for the sake
Of good;
Those
Who are in that love
Abhor merit.

A.9983

Why Less Faith

It is a common
And known thing
That the learned
Have less belief
In a life after death
Than the simple
The reason is
Because they consult
Scientifics,
Which they possesss
In greater abundance
Than others.

A.4760

Truly No Worship

To act
According to the precepts
Of the Lord
Is truly
To worship Him —
Yea, it is
Truly love
And truly faith,
Which may be manifest
To every considerate
Person.

A.10,143

As Burning Fire

Man receives the Divine
Being or Principle
No otherwise than
According to his quality;
On which account
When the Lord appeared
On Mount Sinai
He appeared to the people
As fire burning
Even to the heart of Heaven,
And as darkness,
Clouds, and thick darkness.

A.6832

Solicitude

They have care for the morrow
Who are not content
With their lot,
Who do not
Trust to the Divine
But to themselves,
And who look only
To wordly
And terrestial things
And not to Heavenly;
With such
There universally prevails
Solicitude
About things to come.

A.8478

For Hours and Days

There are
(Amongst the Gentiles
As amongst the Christians)
Both wise and simple;
And in order
That I might be instructed
Concerning the natures
And qualities of each,
It was given me
To discourse with them
For hours and days
Together.

A.2591

For Actual Evils

It is to be observed
That no man suffers
Punishment and torment
In the Other Life
On account of hereditary evils
But for the actual evils
Which he has
Himself committed.

A.966

Upright Judge

The fundamental of charity
Is to act
Rightly and justly
In everything relating
To any duty or office —
As, for example,
If he who is a judge
Punishes a malefactor
According to the laws
(And from zeal)
He is then in charity
Towards his neighbor,
For he wills his amendment,
Thus his good,
And also wills well
To society
And his country.

A.4730

Two Kingdoms

Heaven is divided
Into two Kingdoms, —
In like manner the church;
In the Celestial Kingdom
The essential principle
Is good of love to the Lord;
But in the Spiritual Kingdom
Good of charity
Towards the neighbor.

A.10,245

Procures Power

With respect to combats
And victories over the hells
The case is this:
He who once overcomes them
Overcomes them perpetually
For by victory
He procures to himself
Power over them.

A.8273

Life from God

Man's proprium
Is indeed
A mere dead nothing
Although to him it seems
So real and important,
Yea, as his all.
Whatever lies in him
Is from the life
Of the Lord,
And if this were removed
He would fall down dead
Like a stone.

A.149

Not Instantly

Infants do not come
Into an angelic state
Instantly after death
But they are successively
Introduced thereto
By the knowledges
Of good and truth,
And this according
To all celestial order.

A.2292

Contrary Beliefs

The Sadducees
(Spoken of in Matthew)
Openly denied a resurrection
Yet they did better
Than those at this day
Who profess not to deny
Because it is
And article of faith
And yet deny in their hearts;
So that their professions
Is contrary to their belief,
To their profession.

A.1885

Perfect Perception

Perception is so perfect
With the angels
That they thence
Both know and have known
What is true and good,
What from the Lord
And what from themselves;
And also the quality
Of a stranger
At once on his arrival
And from a single
Idea of him.

A.104

Live from Themselves

Angels perceive that they
Live from the Lord
Although
When not reflecting
On the subject
They know no other
But that they
Live from themselves.

A.155

Lead Gently

Influx through the angels
Takes place
According to man's
Affections
Which they lead gently
And bend to do good
And do not break;
The influx itself
Is tacit
And scarcely perceptible
For it is
Into the interiors
And continually
By freedom.

A.6205

Love The Lord

From love is derived
All Heavenly happiness,
Which is so great
That no degree of it
Admits of description
Or can ever be conceived
By any human idea.
Those who are
Under the influence of love
Love the Lord
From the heart.

A.32

Internal And External

In every church of the lord
There are those
Who are internal men
And those
Who are external;
And the internal are those
Who are in the affection
Of good,
And the external
Those who are
In the affection
Of truth.

A.3447

Not Yet Known

That the whole man
From the head to the heel
Both interiorly and exteriorly
Is nothing but his own
Truth or falsity
Or his own good or evil,
And that the body
Is their external form
Is an arcanum
Which has not yet been known
In the world.

A.10,264

If Heart Dies

The church
Is like the heart
In the natural body,
And so long
As the heart lives
The neighboring
Viscera and members
May live also,
But as soon
As the heart dies,
All and every part
Of the body
Die with it.

A.637

As Heaven's Light

The word
Appears to every one
According to his quality,
When nevertheless
The internal sense
Of the Word
(In respect to its
Literal sense)
Is as the light of Heaven
In respect
To the light of the world.

A.3438

Internal in Heaven

There is an influx
From the Spiritual World
Into the natural
(Thus by the internal man
Into his external)
But not *vice versa*,
For the internal man
Is in Heaven
But the external
In the world.

A.10,057

Good of Innocence

It is to be observed
That the
Good of innocence
Is the very soul
Of Heaven,
Because this good
Is alone receptive
Of love,
Of charity,
And of faith —
Which make the Heavens.

A.10,137

Cannot Preach

Spirits who are only skilled
In the doctrinals
Of faith without love
Are in such coldness of life
And obscurity of light
That they cannot
Even approach
To the first limit
Of the entrance
Into the Heavens,
But fly back with all speed.

A.34

Spiritual Combats

That by wars in the Word
Nothing else is meant
But spiritual combats
May appear evident
From this consideration
That in the Word
Nothing can possibly
Be treated of
But the Lord,
His Kingdom,
And the church,
Since the Word is Divine.

A.1659

Judgments

The good
(As they have received
Divine truths)
Are judged from mercy;
And the evil
As they have not received
Divine truths
Are judged from truth
Thus not from mercy,
For this they have rejected,
And hence also
They reject it
In the Other Life.

A.5068

Pervade Heaven

All the truths
Which are from the Lord
Are not only for men
But also at the same time
For angels,
Inasmuch
As they pervade Heaven
And thus pass to earth.

A.8862

God Dispenses Reward

He who believes in simplicity
That he is able
To do good of himself
And that he will
Receive a reward
In the Other Life
If he is good from himself
Easily admits of being taught
That the good which he does
Is from the Lord
And that He out of mercy
Freely dispenses reward.

A.735

No Other Way

That the
Incomprehensible Divine
Which is called the Father
Is together worshipped
When the Lord
As to the Divine Human
Is worshipped
Is manifest
From the words
Of the Lord Himself
Where He says;
"That He is the Way,
And that no one
Cometh to the Father
But by Him."

A.10,267

Signs from Heaven

When a man
Betakes himself
To evils
(As is the case
With most in youth)
If he feels any anxiety
When he reflects
On what he has done amiss
It is a sign
That he will still receive
Influx from the angels
From Heaven
And it is also a sign
That he will afterwards
Suffer himself
To be reformed;
But if he feels no anxiety
When he reflects
On what he has done amiss
It is a sign
That he is no longer willing
To receive influx
Through the angels
From Heaven.

A.5470

Life of All

The life
Of spirits and angels
Is not supported
By any food
Like that of this world
But by every word
Which comes forth
From the mouth of the Lord,
As the Lord himself teaches.
The fact is
That the Lord alone
Is the life of all.

A.681

Self-Love Destroys

They within the church
Who are principled
In falsity
And at the same time
In self-love
More especially profane
Holy things,
And not so much they
Who are influenced
By any other love;
For self-love
Is the most filthy of all
As being destructive
Of society
And thus
Of the Human Race.

A.2057

Gifted

Whilst man is engaged
In temptation combats
He is at times
Gifted by the Lord
With a state of peace,
And is thus refreshed.

A.1726

Taught by Angels

It has been given
To know of a certainty
That all infants who die
Throughout the whole world
Are raised up by the Lord
And conveyed into Heaven
And are there
Educated and instructed
By the angels
Who have care of them.

A.2289

Does Evil to Neighbor

He who relieves
A poor and indigent villain
Does evil to his neighbor
Through him,
For by the relief
Which he offers,
He confirms him in evil
And supplies him
With opportunity
Of doing evil to others.
It is otherwise with him
Who gives support
To the good.

A.8120

Proprium Vivified

When the things
Of the proprium of man
Are vivified by the Lord
They assume
A beautiful and graceful
Form,
With a variety
According to the life,
To which the celestial
Principle of the Lord
Can be adjoined.

A.154

Faith from Love

The life of faith
Without love
Is like the light of the sun
Without heat
As in the time of winter
When nothing grows
But all things
Are torpid and dead;
Whereas faith
Proceeding from love
Is like the light of the sun
In the time of spring
When all things
Grow and flourish.

A.34

Now Only Few

At this day
There are scarce
Any of the Gentiles
Who may be called wise,
Whereas in ancient times
There were great numbers —
Especially
In the ancient church.

A.2591

Counterfeit Peace

It is believed
That an evil person
Is in peace
When he is in
Gladness and tranquility
Arising from general success
In his concerns;
But this is not peace;
It is the delight
And tranquility of lusts
Which counterfeit
A state of peace.

A.8455

To Be Purified

All worship
Has for its end
That man may be purified
From evils and falses;
Consequently,
That goods and truths
From the Lord
May be implanted in him
And that thus
He may be renegerated.

A.10,022

Externals Removed

It matters not
That a man does not do evil
When he either cannot
Or dare not,
Nor that he does good
From some selfish regard;
Such abstinence from the one
And performance of the other
Have only their origin
In the man's externals,
Which are removed
In the Other Life
Where he is such as his
Thoughts and intentions
Make him.

A.1680

Fountain and Origin

Love
Is from no other source
Than from the Lord,
For He Himself
Is the fountain and origin
Of all celestial
And spiritual love —
Consequently
Of all good thence derived.

A.4352

Inflow Of Life

In regard to the life
Of every one
Whether man, spirit, or angel
It flows in solely
From the Lord
Who is essential Life
And who diffuses Himself
Through the Universal Human
(And even through hell)
Consequently,
Into every individual therein;
But the life which flows in
Is received by everyone
According to his
Prevailing principle —
Good and truth is received
As good and truth by the good,
Whereas good and truth
Is received
As evil and falsity
By the wicked
And is even changed
Into evil and falsity in them.
This is comparatively
As the light of the sun
Which diffuses itself
Into all objects
On the face of the earth
But is received
According to the quality
Of each object
And becomes of a beautiful
Color in beautiful forms
And of an ugly color
In ugly forms . . .
In order that I might know
That such an influx existed
It was given me to discourse
With spirits and angels
Who are attendant on me
And also to feel and perceive
The influx
And this so often
That I am not able
To reckon up all the times.

A.2888

Life Remains

All in hell are such
As have been
In faith so called
Without charity;
But all in Heaven
Are such
As have been principled
In charity;
For everyone's life
Remains with him
After death.

A.5351

Become Enlightened

Those who know little
But possess conscience
Become enlightened
In the Other World
Even so as to become angels,
And then their
Wisdom and intelligence
Are inexpressible.

A.1100

Instantly Perceived

There are many
Who from practice
In the world
Have acquired a habit
Of speaking fairly;
But in the Other Life
It is instantly perceived
Whether the
Mind or intention
Agrees with the words;
If not,
The parties are rejected
Amongst the infernals
Of their own kind
And species.

A.1680

Purification

The states of good spirits
And of angels
Are continually
Changing and perfecting
And thus they are raised
Into the interiors
Of the province
In which they are
And so into nobler functions,
For in Heaven
There is continual
Purification.

                                        A.4803

Angry with God

Those who place merit in works
Love themselves,
And those who love themselves
Despise the neighbor,
Yea, they are angry
With God Himself
If they do not receive
The hoped-for recompense.

                                        A.9976

Two-Fold Origin

The false
Is of a two-fold origin;
The false of doctrine
And the false of evil;
The false of doctrine
Does not consume goods,
For a man may be
In the false of doctrine
And yet in good;
Hence even the Gentiles
Are saved
In all sorts of doctrine,
But the false of evil
Consumes.

                                        A.5149

Pure Love

The life of the Lord
Was love
Towards the whole Human Race,
Which was so great
And of such a nature
As to be nothing but
Pure love.
Against this life of His
Were admitted
Continual temptations
From His earliest childhood
To His last hour
In the world.

                                        A.1690

Descends from Heaven

Love truly conjugial
Is the union
Of two minds,
Which is spiritual union;
And of all spiritual union.
Descends from Heaven;
Hence it is
That love truly conjugial
Is from Heaven.

                                        A.10,168

Many in Number

There are
Certain societies of angels
(And those many in number)
Which have the care
Of infants;
They are chiefly
Of the female sex
Consisting of such
As in the life of body
Have had
The most tender love
Towards infants.

                                        A.2302

Only by Mercy

The reason why infants
(When grown adult)
Are remitted into the state
Of their hereditary evil
Is not that they may
Suffer punishment
But it is in order
To convince them
That of themselves they are
Nothing else but evil
And that by the Lord's mercy
They are raised out of hell
Which appertains to them
Into Heaven;
And that they are
Not in Heaven
By virtue of their own merit
But of the Lord.

A.2308

Like Bright Stars

When the Lord sees good,
The good spirits
Appear to others
(And also to themselves)
Like bright lucid stars
Glittering
According to the quality
Of their charity and faith;
But evil spirits appear
Like globules of coal-fire.

A.1527

Do Not Merit Heaven

Those who believe
That by the goods
Which they do
They merit Heaven
Do good from themselves
And not from the Lord.

A.9974

Cannot Endure Violence

The holy principle of worship
Rooted in early life
Is of such a nature
That it cannot
Endure violence
But must be bent with
Moderation and gentleness;
Such is the case
In regard to the Gentiles
Who during their life
In the body
Had worshipped idols
And yet had lived
In mutual charity.

A.1992

Ardor of Love

Weeping denotes
The ardor of love,
For weeping has relation
Both to sorrow
And to love
And denotes
The highest degree
Of each.

A.3801

Good and Beautiful

Man's proprium
Is mere evil
And when exhibited
To view
Is most deformed;
But when charity
And innocence
From the Lord
Are insinuated
Into the proprium
It then appears
Good and beautiful.

A.164

Due Regard

A man ought to have
Regard for his body, —
To nourish it,
To clothe it,
To let it enjoy
The delights of the world;
But all this
Not for the sake
Of the body
But of the soul.

A.5949

Punishes Itself

When the wicked
Endure punishment
There always
Are angels present
To regulate its degree
And alleviate the pains
Of the sufferers
As much as may be.
They cannot however
Remove them entirely
Because such is the
Equilibrium
Of all things
In the Other Life
That evil punishes itself.

A.967

Meanings

By the Heavens are meant
The angels who are there;
By the church
The men who are true men
Of the church;
And by man in first
Principles
The Lord
As to His Divine Human.

A.10,044

Essential Life

The ground and reason
Why the Word is living
Or alive
And thus gives life
Is because
In a supreme sense
The Lord
Is therein treated of,
And in the inmost sense
His Kingdom,
In which the Lord is all,
And this being the case
There is in the Word
Essential life.

A.3424

The Lord's Kingdom

The New Jerusalem
Is described
As being measured,
And lying four-square,
And its length to be
Equal to its breadth
From which any one may see
That length and breadth
Signify spiritual things
Since the New Jerusalem
Is nothing else
Than the Lord's Kingdom
In the Heavens
And on earth.

A.1613

Not After Death

If man's mind
Has not been opened
Towards interior things
In the life of the body
It cannot be opened
After death.

A.4464

Must Affect Life

Sciences and knowledges
Are of no account
To man in the Other Life
Even though he were
In possession of all the arcana
That ever were revealed
Unless they have tinctured
The life.

A.1197

Self's Interiors

The evil of self-love
Is not
(As it commonly appears)
The external elation
Called pride
But it is hatred
Against the neighbor
And hence a burning desire
Of revenge
And the delight of cruelty;
These are the interiors
Of self-love.

A.4750

Vivified in Reader

The angels say
That the Word of the Lord
Is a dead letter
But that it is vivified
In the reader
By the Lord
According to the faculty
Of each individual,
And that it becomes alive
According to his
Life of charity
And state of innocence —
Which takes place
With endless variety.

A.1776

Evening and Morning

As it is evening
When there is no faith
And morning
When there is faith
Therefore
The Coming of the Lord
Into the world
Is called Morning.

A.22

Must Appear

That man does not live
From himself
Is an eternal truth;
Yet unless he appeared
To live from himself
It would be impossible
For him to live at all.

A.1712

His Risen Body

That the Lord rose again
With the whole body
Which He had in the world
Otherwise than other men
Is a known thing
For He left
Nothing in the sepulchre
Wherefore also
He said to the disciples
Who supposed
When they saw the Lord:
"Why are ye troubled?
Behold My hands
And My feet;
Handle Me and see,
For a spirit
Hath not flesh and bones
As ye see Me have."

A.10,252

Mutual Love

Mutual love
Which reigns in Heaven
Consists in this,
That each loves his neighbor
More than himself;
Hence the whole Heaven
Constitutes as it were
A single man,
All being thus consociated
By mutual love
From the Lord.
Hence too it is
That the felicities of all
Are communicated
To each individual
And those of each individual
To all.

A.2057

Camps of Israel

Essential order
Is what was represented
By the encampments
Of the sons of Israel
In the wilderness,
Thus Heaven itself
Was represented.

A.4236

Proprium Recedes

He who worships the Lord
And gives glory to the Lord
Is in humiliation;
And from him
Who is in humiliation
The proprium recedes;
And in proportion
As the proprium recedes
In the same proportion
The Divine is received.

A.10,646

Charity Teaches

Nothing is more
Necessary for man
Than to know
Whether Heaven be in himself
Or hell;
For in one or the other
He must needs live
To Eternity;
To the intent that he may
Acquire this knowledge
It is necessary
That he should know
What good is and what evil is,
For good
Constitutes Heaven,
And evil constitutes hell;
The doctrine of charity
Taught both.

A.7181

Goods Which Men Do

The goods which men do
From themselves
Are all of them
Not good,
Because they are done
For the sake of self
(Since for the sake
Of reward);
Thus in them
They primarily respect
Themselves.
But the goods which men do
From the Lord
Are all of them good,
Since they are done
For the sake of the Lord
And for the sake
Of the neighbor;
Thus in them the doers
Primarily respect
The Lord and the neighbor.

A.9975

Almost as Angels

The Most Ancient church
(Being celestial)
Was in the good of love
To the Lord
And thence in perception
Of all truth
Insomuch
That the men of that church
Were almost
As the angels;
They also had
Communication with angels
And thence derived
Their perception.

A.4448

From the Divine

Few know from what origin
Conjugial Love exists;
Those who think from the world
Believe that it is
From Nature
But those who think
From Heaven
That it is from the Divine

A.10,167

Become Spiritual

In proportion
As sciences are acquired
With a view to use
Whether for the sake
Of human society
Or the Lord's church on earth,
Or His Kingdom in Heaven,
And more especially
For the Lord's sake
They are more opened
Towards the Lord
And become spiritual.

A.1472

Who Admit the Lord

Around every man
There are hells
Inasmuch
As every one is born
Into evils of every kind,
And where there are evils
There are the hells,
Which
(Unless they were rejected
By the Divine Power
Of the Lord)
Would render it impossible
For any one to be saved.
That this is the case
The Word teaches,
And all those
Comprehend it
Who admit the Lord
Into their life;
And these are they
Who acknowledge Him
And love to live
According to His precepts.

A.10,659

Joy of Conscience

With the regenerate man
There is joy
When he acts
According to conscience,
And anxiety
When forced to do or think
Contrary to it;
But it is not so
With the unregenerate;
For in many instances
He does not know
What conscience is —
Much less
What it is to do anything
Either according
Or contrary to it.

A.977

His Flesh and Blood

All that is holy in Heaven
Proceeds from the Lord's
Divine Human principle
And hence all that is holy
In the church;
Wherefore,
To prevent its violation
The Holy Supper
Was instituted by the Lord,
And there it is said
In express words
That the bread therein
Is His flesh,
And the wine therein
Is His blood.

A.4735

Not True Faith

The faith which regards
Good as derived from self
And not from God
Is not true faith.
Such persons cannot
Receive Heaven
In themselves
For Heaven with man
Is from celestial love
And from true faith.

A.9977

Not More Than One

There cannot possibly exist
More than one
Single true love
Nor more than one
Single true life
Whence flow true joys
And true felicities
Such as are tasted
By the angels in Heaven.

A.33

Spiritual Death

A man who is
Spiritually dead
Is not called dead
Because he is about to die
After the life of the body
But because he will live
The life of death;
For "death"
Is damnation and hell.

A.304

In Heaven or Hell

So long
As a man is only
In the light of the world,
He is in hell;
But when he is
At the same time
In the light of Heaven
He is in Heaven.

A.10,156

Good from Religion

It is one thing
To do good from nature
And another to do it
From Religion;
They cannot be distinguished
By men in the world
Who are not acquainted
With the interiors;
But in the Other Life
They are manifestly discerned,
For in that life
The interiors are manifested —
The thoughts,
The intentions,
And the ends of life
Exhibiting themselves
And being clearly evident.

A.5032

How Man Becomes Man

From the internal sense
It is manifest
How the case was
With the Lord —
Namely,
That His external man
Or Human Essence
Was conjoined to the
Divine Essence by degrees
According to the
Multiplication
And fructification
Of knowledges.
It is not possible
For any one (as man)
To be conjoined to Jehovah
Or the Lord
Except by knowledges;
For by knowledges
Man becomes man.
This was the case
With the Lord.

A.1616

The Lord's Divine

It is to be noted
That whatsoever
Represented
The Lord Himself,
This also
Represented Heaven
For the Divine
(Proceeding
From the Lord)
Received by the angels
Makes Heaven.
The angels themselves
Do not constitute Heaven
But as to the Divine
Which they receive
From the Lord.

A.10,151

Raised into Heaven

They who have lived
In love to the Lord
And in charity
Towards their neighbor
Retain all the evils
Of their lives;
But in them
They are tempered
By the good principles
Which they have received
From the Lord
Through the life of charity
During their abode
In the world;
And thus they are elevated
Into Heaven.

A.2116

Evil Delights

They with whom the love of self
And of the world
Make the life,
Will good
To themselves alone,
And not to others
Except for the sake
Of themselves;
And whereas their life
Is from hell,
They despise others
In comparison with themselves.
They are angry with them
If they do not
Favor themselves
They hate them,
Burn with revenge
Against them,
Yea, are desirous to commit
All outrage towards them;
These things at length
Become the delights of their life.

A.10,742

Would Not Exchange

Angles have declared to me
That if they could possess
All the palaces
Throughout the whole earth
They would not
Exchange their own for them.
What is of stone,
Mortar, and wood
Is to them dead;
But what is from the Lord
And from essential
Life and light —
This, they say, is alive
And the more so
As they enjoy it
With all fullness of sense.

A.1628

Good Given by Truths

Every good which man has
From the Lord
Is given him by truths,
For man is born
Into mere ignorance
And when he advances
In age,
He has of himself
Mere thick darkness.
In things spiritual,
For he knows nothing
Concerning God,
Concerning the Lord,
Concerning Heaven and hell,
Concerning life after death.
What he knows from himself
Relates to the world
And to himself;
And he calls that good
Which in the world
Is in favor of himself
And he calls that true
Which confirms it.

A.10,661

Order of Influx

That every good is in portion
Of those
Who worship the Lord
From internal motives
Is manifest
From the order of things;
For from the Lord proceeds
Whatever is celestial;
From this all that is spiritual,
And from what is spiritual
All that is natural;
This is the order
Of all created existences,
And hence is derived
The order of influx.

A.1096

Love Grieving

That weeping is an effect
Of grief and love
Is well known;
Consequently,
It is an effect of mercy;
On this account
The Divine Love
Is called mercy.

A.5480

Take Heed

Let every one
Who is within the church
Take heed to himself
Lest he deny the Lord
And also lest he
Deny His Divine
For to that denial
Heaven is closed
And hell is opened.

A.10,033

The Lord So Rose

No man
Rises again in the body
With which he was clothed
In the world;
But the Lord so rose
Because He glorified His body
Or made it Divine
While He was in the world.

A.5078

Wars and Rumors

By "hearing of wars
And rumors of wars"
Signifies
There would exist
Disputes and litigations
Concerning truths,
Which are "wars"
In the spiritual sense.

A.3353

Not Hurtful

To believe
That they are rewarded
If they do good
Is not hurtful with those
Who are in innocence
As with infants
And with the simple,
But to
Confirm themselves therein
When they become adults
Is hurtful,
For man is initiated
Into good
By respecting reward
And he is
Deterred from evil
By respecting
Punishments.

A.9982

Such as the Love

What anyone does from love
Remains inscribed
On his heart,
For love is the fire
Of life;
Thus is the life
Of every one;
Hence,
Such as the love is,
Such is the life;
And such as the life is,
Such is the whole man
As to soul
And as to body.

A.10,740

Appropriates

The man who supposes
That he lives from himself
Is in the false,
And in consequence
Appropriates to himself
Every thing evil and false,
Which he would never do
Were he to believe
According to the real truth
Of the case.

A.150

Love and Faith

There are two things
Which make the life of man,
Love and faith;
Love makes the life
Of his will,
And faith the life of his
Understanding;
Hence such as the love is
And such as the faith is,
Such is the life.

A.10,714

The Very Word

The very Word itself
Which is the internal sense
Does not at all treat
Of kings and people
But of things
Celestial and spiritual
Appertaining
To the Lord's Kingdom —
Consequently,
Of things relating
To goodness and truth.

A.2069

Holy Fear

Holy fear
Is not a fear
On account of
Hell and damnation
But is an aversion
Of doing or thinking
Anything against the Lord
Or against our neighbor;
Thus it is an aversion
Of doing or thinking
Anything contrary
To goodness and truth.

A.2826

Conjugial Freedom

What is done
From a principle
Of love truly conjugial
This is done from freedom
On both sides
For all freedom
Is from love,
And each party has freedom
When one loves
What the other thinks
And what the other wills.

A.10,173

From God Alone

When the Lord
Raises up to life
Or regenerates man
He permits him
At first to suppose
That he does good
And speaks truth
From himself,
Inasmuch
As at that time
He is incapable
Of conceiving
Otherwise,
Nor can he otherwise
Be led to believe,
And afterwards
To perceive
That all goodness
And truth
Are from the Lord alone.

A.39

Spiritual Cities Seen

Besides paradisical objects
There are cities
Exhibited to view
With magnificent palaces
Contiguous to each other
Splendid in their colors
And of an architecture
Surpassing
All the powers of art.
This is the less surprising
Since cities were seen also
By the prophets
When their interior sight
Was open,
And this so plainly
That nothing in the world
Could be plainer.
Thus John
Saw the New Jerusalem.

A.1626

Holy Principle

Heaven is in
The internal sense
Of the Word,
And the internal sense
Corresponds
To the external sense;
Wherefore when the Word
Is read by man
The angels who are
Attendant upon him
Perceive it in
The spiritual sense;
Hence a holy principle
From the angels
Flows in.

A.10,687

In His Divine

The Lord is present
With the angels of Heaven
And with
The men of the church
Not in their proprium
But in what is
Of Himself
Appertaining to them —
Thus in what is
Divine.

A.10,157

Continual Worship

By worship
In the internal sense
Is signified
All conjunction
By love and charity.
Man is
Continually in worship
When he is
In love and charity.

A.1618

Two Fires

There are two
Fires of life
Appertaining to man;
One is the love of self,
The other
Is the love of God;
Those who are
In love of self
Cannot be
In love to God
Since they are opposites.

A.10,038

Life of Love

The Most Ancient Church
Acknowledged no faith
Distinct from love itself;
The celestial angels also
Do not know what faith is
Except it be of love;
And the universal Heaven
Is of love —
No other life
Being existent in Heaven
But the life of love.

A.32

To Death or Life

It is the last judgment
To every one
Immediately on his death;
For he then passes
Into the Other Life
(On his coming again
Into the life
Which he had in the body)
He is judged
Either to death
Or to life.

A.1850

Continually Remembers

The case of faith is this:
He that receives it
(And has it)
Is continually
In remembrance of the Lord
Even when he is
Thinking and conversing
On other subjects,
And likewise
When he is engaged
In his public, private,
Or domestic duties
Although he is ignorant
At the time
That he remembers the Lord.

A.5130

Man Descended

In process of time
Wisdom retired
From inmost things
To outermost,
And man
Removed himself from Heaven;
And at length descended
Even to the dust
Of the earth,
Wherein wisdom
Is now made to consist.

A.3432

Babylon

It is well known
That by Babylon are signified
Those who have turned aside
All worship of the Lord
To the worship of self
And who
(In consequence thereof)
Are in a profane
Internal principle
Whilst they are
In a holy external.

A.4748

Lord's Presence

The Lord is indeed
Present with every man;
But in proportion
As man is distant
From charity,
In the same proportion
The presence of the Lord
(So to speak)
Is more absent,
Or the Lord
Is more remote.

A.981

By Affections

Man believes
That goods and truths
Flow in immediately
Out of Heaven,
Thus without mediums
Appertaining to man,
But he is much deceived;
The Lord leads every one
By his affections
And thereby bends him
By a tacit Providence.

A.4364

Word Holy from Within

He who is intelligent
May know
From consideration
That the Word is most holy
And that the literal sense
Is holy
From the internal sense,
But that separated from it,
It is not holy;
For the literal sense
Separated from the internal
Is as the external of man
Separate from his internal.
Which is an image
Of no life.

A.10,276

The Holiest Name

Jehovah
Is a name most holy
And belongs
Only to the church,
Whereas
God is not so holy
Inasmuch as
Every nation had gods
And therefore
The name "god"
Was not so holy;
It was not allowed
Anyone to name
The name Jehovah
But those who had
Knowledge
Of the true faith
Whereas everyone
Might name the name of God.

A.624

Extinguishes Delights

Self-love communicates
Nothing to others
But extinguishes
And suffocates
The delights and felicities
Of others.
Whatever delight flows
From others into those
Who are in self-love
They take to themselves,
Center it in themselves,
Turn it into the defilement
Of self,
And prevent
Its further propogation;
Thus they destroy everything
That tends to
Unanimity and consociation,
Whence result disunion
And consequent destruction.

A.2057

Only from God

There is a life
Only in those things
Which are of the Lord
As must be evident
To every one who reflects
That there is no vitality
In anything unconnected
With Eternal Life
Or which does not
Regard Eternal Life.
The life which is not eternal
Is not life
But in a little while
Perishes.

A.726

Angels Esteem Use

The angels,
Who are principled
In the science
Of all knowledges,
And that in such a manner
That scarce a thousandth part
Can be unfolded
To man's apprehension,
Yet esteem knowledges
As nothing
In comparison to use.

A.1472

Scarcely See Evils

Those who are in charity
Scarcely see another's evils
But observe all
That is good and true in him,
And what is evil and false
They interpret favorably;
Such are all the angels,
And this disposition
They derive from the Lord.

A.1079

No Avail

The work of repentance
Which is done in a free state
Is of avail
But that which is done
In a state of compulsion
Is not of avail;
A state of compulsion
Is a state of sickness,
A state
Of dejection of mind
In consequence
Of misfortunes,
A state of imminent death.

                                        A.8392

Evil Result

When a person
Thinks to merit salvation
By works
And confirms himself
In such an idea,
Self-merit.
Self-justification,
And self-confidence
Are the evils
Thence resulting.

                                        A.1679

Cannot Be Together

It is according to order
That in the Other Life
All be consociated
According to the life
Which they have
Acquired to themselves
In the world;
The evil with the evil
And the good with the good;
Hence it is not possible
That the evil and good
Can be together.

                                        A.8700

Every World Spiritual

As every particular expression
In the Word
Is from the Lord
And consequently contains
A Divine principle,
It is evident
That there cannot be
A single word or iota in it
Which does not signify
And involve
Something spiritual.

                                        A.771

Who Is Neighbor

They are the neighbor
Who are in good;
Whereas they who are in evil
Are indeed neighbor
But altogether
In another respect;
And this being the case
Good is to be done to them
In another way.

                                        A.6708

Not in the Church

They who are
In external worship
Without internal
Love truths
Not for the sake of truth
But for the sake
Of gain in the world;
Thus, they do not love
To do truths
Except for the sake
Of themselves,
Or that they may be seen;
These are not in the church.
But out of it.

                                        A.10,683

Ascends Towards Heaven

The sense of the letter
In its ascent towards Heaven
Is put off,
And instead thereof
Another Heavenly sense
Takes place,
Insomuch
That this latter sense
Cannot be known
To be from the former;
For they who are in Heaven
Are in the idea
That all things of the Word
In the internal sense
Treat of the Lord.

A.3382

Continually Born

The age of infancy
Is as it were an egg
For the age of childhood
And the age of childhood
Is as it were an egg
For the age
Of adolescence and youth,
And this latter as an egg
For adult age.
Thus man is as it were
Continually born.

A.4378

Express Arcana

No other
Historical circumstances
Are recorded,
Nor in any other order,
Nor other expressions used
Than such as
In the internal sense
Might express arcana.

A.1468

Come in After Death

With all who receive
Love and faith from the Lord
There is Heaven;
Both with angels
And with men;
Wherefore, they who have
Heaven in themselves
Whilst they live in the world
Come into Heaven
After death.

A.10,717

Angelic Faith

The appropriation
Of Divine good
And Divine truth
From the Lord
Cannot be given
Except with those
Who acknowledge
The Divine of the Lord.
For this is the first
And the very essential
Of all things which are
Of faith in the church;
For Heaven cannot be
Unclosed to others
Since the whole Heaven
Is in that faith.

A.10,033

Spiritual Names

In the names
Which occur in the Word
There is nothing spiritual
Unless they signify
Things of the church
And Heaven
For these things
Are spiritual.

A.10,329

He Prayed for All

The Lord's
Whole life in the world
(From His earliest childhood)
Was a continual temptation
And continual victory,
The close of which was
When He prayed on the Cross
For His enemies —
Consequently for all
That dwell on the face
Of the whole earth.

A.1690

Heaven of Internals

The Heaven
Nearest to the Lord
Consists of human internals;
This however is above
The inmost angelic Heaven;
Wherefore these internals
Are the habitations
Of the Lord Himself.
The whole Human Race
Is thus
Most intimately present
Under the eyes of the Lord.

A.1999

Two Lights

There are two lights:
One which is of the world
From the sun;
The other
Which is of Heaven
From the Lord.
In the light of the world
There is nothing
Of intelligence,
But in the light of Heaven
There is.

A.4405

No Other Lord

That the "land"
Or Heavenly Kingdom
Belongs to the Lord alone
Appears from what
Has been abundantly shown —
That is,
That there is no other
Lord of Heaven;
And since He is
Lord of Heaven
He is also
Lord of the church.

A.1614

Stars Shall Fall

"The stars shall fall
From heaven"
Signifies
That the knowledges
Of good and truth
Shall perish.
Nothing else
Is signified in the Word
By "stars"
Whenever they are named.

A.4060

Proprium Dispersed

The human proprium
Is altogether evil and false,
And so long as it
Continues active,
Man is in a state of death,
But when he undergoes
Temptations
Is becomes dispersed,
Or in other words
Loosened and attempered
By truths and goods
From the Lord.

A.731

Image of Heaven

A man who is in
Correspondence —
That is,
Who is principled
In love to the Lord
And in charity
Towards his neighbor,
(And thence in faith)
As to his spirit is in Heaven
And as to his body
In the world;
And inasmuch
As he thus acts
In unity with the angels
He is also an image
Of Heaven.

A.3634

Always Being Perfected

The regeneration of man
Commences in the world
And continues to Eternity,
For man,
When he becomes an angel,
Is always
Being perfected.

A.10,048

From the Heart

A man may utter from memory
Many truths from the Word
But unless they are produced
By love and charity.
Holiness cannot be
Predicated of them;
But if so produced
They are at the same time
Acknowledged and believed
And thus spoken
From the heart.

A.724

Are His Seed

They are "born of God"
Who are principled
In love
And faith thence derived;
And as they are
"Born of God"
They are called
Sons of God
And are His seed,
And receive
The Heavenly Kingdom.

A.1608

Gentile Nations

The Gentile nations
Who are without the church
And who are principled
In good
Are saved
Alike with those
Who are within the church.

A.3380

Three Things

There are three things
Appertaining to man
Which follow
In succesive order;
Those three are called
Celestial, spiritual,
And natural.
The celestial
Is the good of love
To the Lord;
The spiritual
The good of charity
Towards the neighbor;
And the natural
Thence derived
The good of faith.

A.9992

Divine Image

When the subject
Treated of in the Word
Is the regeneration
Of man,
In the supreme sense
The Glorification
Of the Lord's Human
Is treated of,
For the regeneration
Of man
Is the image of the
Lord's Glorification.

A.10,042

Conjugial Holiness

Marriages are holy
And to do
Violence to them
Is to do violence
To that which is holy;
Consequently,
Adulteries are profane
For since the delight
Of conjugial love
Descends from Heaven
The delight of adultery
Ascends from hell.

A.10,174

Blessed Ones

Infernal torments
Are not (as some suppose)
The stings of conscience,
For those who are in hell
Have no conscience.
And consequently
Cannot be so tormented;
For such as have had
Conscience
Are among the blessed.

A.965

Oppose and Hinder

The mercy of the Lord
Is perpetually attendant
On every man,
For the Lord
Wills to save all men
How many soever they be;
But this mercy
Cannot flow in
Until evils are removed,
For evils
And the falses
Thence derived
Oppose and hinder.

A.8307

Nation's Quality

The internal sense
Is not at all concerned
About the memoirs
And historical transactions
Relating to any nation,
But only about its quality
As to those things
Which regard the church.

A.4864

Occasions Darkness

As soon as the light
Of Heaven
Which is from the Lord
Flows into any hell
It occasions there
Darkness and thick darkness.
From this consideration
It may now be manifest
That the Lord
Appears to every one
According to his quality
Because according
To reception.

A.6832

Truths Multiplied

So far as evils
And the falses of evil
Are removed,
So far the truths
Which are from good
Are multiplied,
Since nothing else but evils
And the falses thence derived
Oppose truths flowing in
From the Lord
And multiplying themselves
In man;
Wherefore,
So far as evils and falses
Are removed,
So far truths
Succeed in their place.

A.10,675

Book of Memory

He who does not know
From the internal sense
What the book of life is
(Also what are the books
Out of which the dead
Are to be judged)
Cannot form any other idea
Than that in Heaven
There are such books,
And that in them are written
The actions of all whereof
The memory is thus preserved,
When yet by books
Are not meant books
But the remembrance
Of all things
That have been done;
For every one
Carries along with him
Into the Other Life
The memory of his actions —
Thus, the book of his life.

A.8620

Heaven Builded

By the Divine Truth
Proceeding
From the Divine Good
Of the Lord
Heaven is builded
And the church is builded;
And by it
All who are in the church
Are regenerated;
These are the things
Which are described
By the sacrifices
And burnt-offerings
And their ceremonials.

A.10,057

False Principles

Persuasions or principles
Grounded and rooted
In what is false
Impede
All Divine operations;
And unless they are
First extirpated
It is impossible for man
To become regenerate.

A.635

Treats of All Men

The Word of the Lord
Is so written
That wherever it speaks
Of one person
It treats of all men
And of every individual,
With a difference
According to the
Disposition of each;
This being the universal
Sense of the Word.

A.838

Descended

In the Word
All things
Are representative
Of spiritual
And celestial things
And are real
Correspondences;
For the Word
Descended from Heaven
And consequently
In its origin
It is Divine celestial
And spiritual.

A.4434

Protection

I have sometimes
Been surrounded
By thousands
To whom it was permitted
To spit forth their venom
And infest me
By all possible methods
Yet without being able
To hurt
A single hair of my head
So secure was I
Under the Lord's
Protection.

A.59

Such His Worship

The church
Is where the Word is
(And from the Word);
And worship is
From those things
Which are in the Word;
Hence such as is
Man's understanding
Of the Word,
Such is the church in him
And such his worship.

A.10,707

Man Is Governed

Man is altogether ignorant
That he is governed
Of the Lord alone
By angels and spirits
And that with every one
There are at least
Two spirits and two angels.
By spirits
Man has comunication
With the World of Spirits
And by angels
With Heaven.

A.50

From Heaven or Hell

Whatsoever man thinks
And whatsoever he wills
And whatsoever he believes
And whatsoever he loves
Is either from Heaven
Or from hell.

A.10,741

Divine Necessity

I have frequently
Discoursed with spirits
Concerning the Word
And the necessity that
By the Divine Providence
Of the Lord
Some revelation should exist;
For a revelation or Word
Is the common vessel
Receptive of things
Spiritual and celestial
And thus effective
Of conjunction
Between Heaven and earth,
Which otherwise would have been
In a state of disjunction,
To the utter
Ruin and destruction
Of the Human Race.

A.1775

External Worship

Man during his abode
In the world
Ought not to omit
The practice of
External worship,
For by external worship
Things internal
Are excited;
And by external worship
Things external are kept
In a state of sanctity,
So that internal things
Can enter by influx.

A.1618

Therein Is the Lord

With respect to the Divine
In the Word
The case is this:
The essential Divine
Is in the supreme sense
Of the Word
Because therein is the Lord.

A.3439

Divine Cloud

The Word
As to the external sense
Is in a cloud
Because human minds
Are in darkness;
Wherefore,
Unless the Word
Were in a cloud
It would scarcely
Be understood by any one
And the holy things
Of the internal sense
Would be profaned
By the wicked in the world.

A.5922

New Church

By a new Heaven
And new earth
Which was to succeed
Instead of the former
Nothing else is signified
But a New Church
Internal and external.

A.3355

Divine Truth

In an eminent sense
The Word
Is the Divine Truth
By reason that everything
Which really exists
And which is anything
Is from the Divine Truth;
Therefore, it is said
In David:
"By the Word of Jehovah
Were the Heavens made
And by the breath
Of His mouth
All the host of them."

A.9987

Continually Uplifted

He who lives the life of faith
Does daily
The work of repentance,
For he reflects on the evils
Appertaining to himself,
He acknowledges them,
Bewares of them,
Supplicates the Lord
For aid;
For man is continually
Lapsing of himself
But is continually raised
By the Lord.

A.8391

Free-Verse Poems from Swedenborg's *Apocalypse Revealed* Rev. 21, 22

The New Heaven

"And I saw a New Heaven
And a new earth."
These words signify
That a New Heaven was formed
From among Christians
By the Lord
Which at this day is called
The Christian Heaven
Where they are
Who had worshipped
The Lord
And lived according
To His Commandments.

R.876

Where Angels Dwell

By a New Heaven and new earth
Is not meant the natural heaven
Visible to the eye
Nor the natural earth
Inhabited by men
But the spiritual Heaven
Is meant
And the earth
Belonging to the Heaven.

R.876

Jerusalem the Church

It is said that John
Saw the holy city Jerusalem
Coming down from God
Out of Heaven
Prepared as a Bride
Adorned for her husband
By which is not meant
Any Jerusalem coming down
But the church,
For the church upon earth
Comes down from the Lord
Out of the Angelic Heaven.

R.876

In the New Heaven

In the New Christian Heaven
Are all those who
From the first formation
Of the Christian church
Worshipped the Lord
And lived according
To His Commandments
And who therefore were
In charity
And at the same time
In faith.

R.876

The New Church

"I, John, saw the holy city
New Jerusalem
Coming down from God
Out of Heaven"
Signifies a New Church
To be established
By the Lord
At the end of the former church
Which will be consociated
With the New Heaven
In Divine truths
As to doctrine and life.

R.879

By a New Name

It is the New Church
Which is meant by Jerusalem
Which shall be called
By a new name
Which the mouth of Jehovah
Shall name
And which shall be
A crown of glory
In the hand of the Lord
And a royal diadem
In the hand of God.

R.880

Prepared as a Bride

It is said that John
Saw the holy city
New Jerusalem
Prepared as a Bride
Adorned for her Husband
From which it is evident
That by Jerusalem
Is meant the church
And that he saw it first
As a city
And afterwards
As an espoused virgin.

A.881

The Bridegroom

The Lord is called
The Bridegroom and Husband,
And the church
The Bride and Wife,
And this marriage
Is like the marriage
Of good and truth

R.881

All Things New

"Behold I make all things new."
That the former Heaven
And the former earth
And the former church
With all things in them
Should perish
And that He should create
A New Heaven
Together with a new earth
And a New Church
And that they may know this
Of a certainty
And bear it in remembrance
Because the Lord Himself
Testified and said it.

R.886

On the Throne

By Him who sat on the throne
Is meant the Lord.
The reason why the Lord
Spake from the throne
Is because He said,
"Behold, I make all things new,"
By which is signified
That He was about
To execute
The Last Judgment,
And then to create
A New Heaven
And a new earth
And a New Church.

R.886

Alpha and Omega

"I am the Alpha and Omega"
Signifies that they may know
That the Lord is the God
Of Heaven and earth,
And that all things
In the Heavens and earths
Were made by Him
And are governed
By His Divine Providence
And are done
According to it.

R.888

The Lamb's Wife

By the "Bride of the Lamb's Wife"
Is signified the New Church
Which will be conjoined
With the Lord
Through the Word.
That church is called a Bride
In reference to its establishment
And a Wife in reference
To its being fully established.

R.895

Wall of the City

When by the holy city Jerusalem
Is meant
The Lord's New Church
As to doctrine,
By its wall
Nothing else is meant
But the Word
In its literal sense,
For that sense
Defends the spiritual sense
Which lies concealed within
Just as a wall
Defends a city.

R.898

Foundations of the Earth

In the Word
"Foundation of the earth"
Are sometimes named,
And by them
Are not to be understood
The foundations of the earth
But the foundations
Of the church,
For the earth
Signifies the church;
And the foundations of the church
Are no other
Than what are derived
From the Word
And are called doctrinals.

R.902

Length and Breadth

The length
Of the city of Jerusalem
Signifies
The good of the church
And the breadth
The truth of the church.

R.906

Consociated with Angels

Every man in goods and truths
Of the church
Is consociated
With angels of Heaven.
By the interiors of his mind
He dwells with them.
They who are in good of love
In the east and west of Heaven
And they who are
In truths of wisdom
In the north and south
Of Heaven.

R.906

Good of Love

"The city was pure gold
Like unto clear glass."
These words signify
That everything appertaining
To the New Church
Is the good of love
Flowing in together
With light out of Heaven
From the Lord.

R.912

No Temple Therein

"I saw no temple therein
For its temple is the Lord."
These words signify
That in the New Church
There will not be any external
Separated
From what is internal
Because the Lord Himself
In His Divine Humanity
(From whom is derived
The all of the church)
Is alone approached,
Worshipped, and adored.

R.918

Glory of the Lord

By the glory of the Lord
Which enlightens
Is meant the Divine truth,
And because that light
Is from the Lord
It is said
That the lamp thereof
Is the Lamb.

R.919

Walking in the Light

By walking in the light
Of the New Jerusalem
Is signified
To perceive and see
Divine truths
From interior illumination.

R.920

Glory and Honor

By bringing glory and honor
Into the New Jerusalem
Is signified
To confess the Lord
And ascribe to Him
All the good and truth
Which they possess.

R.921

Opened Gates

"And the gates of it
Shall not be shut by day."
These words signify
That they will be
Continually received
Into the New Jerusalem
Who are in truths
Derived from good of love.

R.922

Nothing That Defiles

"There shall not enter
Anything that defileth"
Signifies
That no one will be received
Into the Lord's New Church
Who adulterates the goods
And falsifies the truths
Of the Word.

R.924

Lamb's Book of Life

"They who are written
In the Lamb's book of life"
Signifies
That no others
Will be received
Into the New Church
Which is the New Jerusalem
But they who believe
In the Lord
And live according
To His Commandments.

R.925

The Pure River

"And He showed me a pure river
Of water of life
Clear as crystal
Proceeding
Out of the throne of God
And of the Lamb."
These words signify
The Apocalypse
Now opened and explained
As to its spiritual sense
Where Divine truths
Are revealed in abundance
From the Lord
For those who will be
In His New Church.

R.932

Tree of Life

"In the midst
Was the Tree of Life."
This signifies
That in the inmost
Of the truths of doctrine
And thence of life
In the New Church
Is the Lord
In His Divine love
From whom flow all the goods
Which man there does
Apparently
As from himself.
"In the midst" signifies
In the inmost.

R.933

In Divine Love

In the New Church
Is the Lord
In His Divine love
From whom flow all the goods
Which man does
Apparently from himself.
This is the case with those
Who immediately
Approach the Lord
And shun evils
Because they are sins
Thus who will be
In the Lord's New Church
Which is the New Jerusalem.

R.933

No More Curse

"And there shall be
No more curse."
By there being no more curse
Is signified
That no evil or falsity
Will be in the New Jerusalem

R.937

God's Love Enters

In proportion
As evils with their delights
Are removed,
In the same proportion
The love of God enters
Which is universal
Towards all,
And in this case
Man is withdrawn from hell
And led into Heaven.
Man must do this
In the world.

R.937

The Lord's Name

By the "name" of the Lord
Being in their foreheads
Is signified
That the Lord loves them
And turns them to Himself.
By His "name"
Is signified
The Lord Himself.

R.938

No Night There

"And there shall be
No night there
And they need no lamp
Neither light of the sun;
For the Lord of God
Giveth them light."
These words signify
That in the New Jerusalem
There will not be
Any falsity of faith
And that men there
Will not be knowledges
Concerning God
Which is from
Their own intelligence
But from the Lord alone.

R.940

Holy Prophets

"The Lord God
Of the holy prophets
Signifies the Lord
From whom is the Word
Of both convenants
For by the prophets
Are signified
They who teach truths
From the Word
And (in an abstract sense)
The doctrine of the truth
Of the church
And in an extensive sense
The Word itself.

R.943

I Come Quickly

"Behold I come quickly"
Signifies that the Lord
Will certainly come.
By "quickly" is signified
Certainly,
And by "coming" is signified
That He will come
Not in Person
But in the Word
In which He will appear
Of His New Church.

R.944

Blessed Is He

"Blessed is he who keeps
The words of this book"
Signifies that He will give
Eternal Life
To those who will keep and do
The truths of doctrine
Contained in this book
Now opened by the Lord.

R.944

Worship God

That John thought
That the angel
Who was sent to him
Was God Himself
Is evident for it is said
That he fell down
To worship at His feet,
But that this
Was not the case
Appears from the next verse
Where the angel says
"I am thy fellow servant.
Worship God.

R.945

Angel Brethren

The angels of Heaven
Are not to be worshipped
Because nothing Divine
Belongs to them
But they are associated
With men
As brethren with brethren.
The Lord alone
Is to be worshipped.

R.946

Seal Not

"Seal not the words
Of the prophecy
Of this book" signifies
That the Apocalypse
Is not to be shut but opened
And that this is
Absolutely necessary
At the end of the church.
By "Seal not the sayings
Of this prophecy" is signified
That the Apocalypse
Must not be shut.

R.947

Apocalypse

The Apocalypse
Is a sealed book or shut
So long as not explained.
By the sayings of this prophecy
Are meant the truths
Of doctrine in this book
Opened by the Lord.
This is necessary
At the end of the church
That some may be saved.
From these considerations
It may appear
That by "Seal not the sayings
Of this prophecy"
Is signified
That the Apocalypse
Must not be shut
But that it must be opened.

R.947

Holy Separations

In porportion as goods
Are taken away
From anyone in evils,
So much the more
Is He in evils,
And in proportion
As truths are taken away
From anyone in falses
So much the more
Is he in falses,
And (on the other hand)
In proportion
As evils are taken away
From anyone in goods
So much the more
Is he in goods,
And in proportion as falses
Are taken away from anyone
Who is in truths
So much the more
He is in truths.

R.948

Charity and Faith

That charity and faith
Are not from man
But from the Lord
Is well known;
And since they are
From the Lord
They are
According to conjunction
With Him.

R.949

The Lord's Reward

"My reward is with Me."
These words signify
That He Himself is Heaven
And the felicity
Of Eternal life
For reward is intrinsic
Beatitude
Which is called peace
And consequently
External joy also.
These are solely from the Lord,
And the things
Which are from the Lord
Not only are from Him
But also are Himself.

R.949

God the Creator

The Lord
Is the God of Heaven and earth
And by Him all things
In the Heavens
And in the earths
Were made
And are governed
By His Divine Providence
And happen
According to it.

R.950

Blessed Are They

"Blessed are they
That do His Commandments."
They enjoy Eternal felicity
Who live according to the
Lord's Commandments
To the end
That they may be
In the Lord
And the Lord in them
By love,
And in the New Church
By knowledges
Concerning Him.

R.951

Angelic Power

Such power
Have the angels in Heaven
That if they only will a thing
They obtain it
But yet they do not
Will anything
But what has relation to use.

R.951

Before the World

"I Jesus
Have sent Mine angel
To testify unto to you
These things in the churches"
Signified a testification
Before the whole
Christian world
That it is true
That the Lord alone
Made manifest the things
Described in this book
And also the things
Which are now
Laid open.

R.953

Lord Jesus

The reason why the Lord
Names Himself Jesus
Is that all
In the Christian world
May know
That the Lord Himself
Who was in the world
Manifested the things
Which are described
In this book
As also the things
Which are now laid open.

R.953

Spirit and Bride

"The Spirit and the Bride
Say, Come" signifies
That Heaven and the church
Desire the Lord's Coming.
By the Spirit
Is signified Heaven.
By the Bride the church,
And by saying, "Come,"
Is signified to desire
The Lord's Coming.

R.955

The Church

By the church
Here called the Bride
Is not meant the church
Consisting of those
Who are in falses of faith
But the church
Consisting of those
Who are
In truths of faith
For these are desirous of light,
Consequently
Of the Lord's Coming.

R.955

Should Pray

That he who knows
Anything of the Lord's Coming
And of the New Heaven
And New Church
Consequently,
Of the Lord's Kingdom
Should pray
That it may come
And that he who desires truths
Should pray that the Lord
Would come with light
And that he who loves truths
Will then receive them
From the Lord
Without any labor of his own.

R.956

The Kingdom

The Lord's Kingdom
Is the church
Which makes one with Heaven
Wherefore it is now said
"Let him that heareth
Say, Come
And let him that is athirst
Come."
To thirst signifies
To desire truths.

R.956

Dare Not Add

To hear the words
Of the prophecy of this book
Signifies to read and know
The truths of doctrine
In this book
Now opened by the Lord.
By adding to them is signified
To add anything
To destroy those truths.

R.957

Mystic Book

The Apocalypse
Has been hitherto
Like a closed or mystic book
Wherefore anyone may see
That nothing should be added
Or taken away
Which destroys
The truths of doctrine
In this book
Now opened by the Lord.

R.957

The Word

The Word which was dictated
From the Lord
Passed through the Heavens
Of His Celestial Kingdom
And the Heavens
Of His Spiritual Kingdom
And thus came to man
By whom it was written.

R.959

Purely Divine

The Word
As it passed through the Heavens
Of the Lord's Celestial Kingdom
Was Divine Celestial,
And as it passed
Through the Heavens
Of the Lord's Spiritual Kingdom
Was Divine Spiritual,
And when it came to man
It became Divine Natural;
Hence it is
That the natural sense
Contains in itself
The spiritual sense,
And this the celestial sense
And both a sense purely Divine.

R.959

Heavenly Faith

By not adding or taking away
Anything written
In the Apocalypse
Is meant in Heaven
That not anything
Is to be added or taken away
From the truths of doctrine
Concerning the Lord
And concerning
Faith in Him.

R.959

Approach Lord Alone

They who do not
Immediately approach
The Lord
Cannot see any truth
From the Word.
To take away their part
Out of the holy city
Signifies
Out of the New Church
Which is
The holy Jerusalem
For no one is received
Into it
Who does not approach
The Lord alone.

R.958

His Divine Humanity

The Lord
Who revealed the *Apocalypse*
And has now opened it
Testifies the glad tidings
That He comes
In His Divine Humanity
Which He took upon Him
In the world
And Glorified.

R.960

The Lord's Angel

"I, Jesus
Have sent Mine angel
To testify unto you
These things in the churches."
These words signify
A testification
Before the whole
Christian world
That it is true
That the Lord alone
Manifested the things
Written in this book
Which are now laid open.

R.960

The Divine Testimony

By "He who testifieth
These things"
Is meant the Lord
Who revealed the Apocalypse
And has now laid it open.
He here declares
His advent,
His Kingdom,
And His spiritual marriage
With the church

R.960

Jesus Only

That the Lord will come
In His Divine Humanity
Which He took upon Him
And Glorified in the world
Is plain
From this circumstance
That He names Himself
"Jesus"
And says that He
Is the Root and Offspring
Of David.

R.960

Recommended Swedenborg Foundation Publications and Films on Related Subjects

Books about Swedenborg

THE SWEDENBORG EPIC: The Life and Works of Emanuel Swedenborg.
By Cyriel Odhner Sigstedt (Swedenborg Society, London)
The classic biography of Swedenborg

THE ESSENTIAL SWEDENBORG
By Sig Synnestvedt
A presentation of the basic elements of Swedenborg's thought.

THE PRESENCE OF OTHER WORLDS: The Psychological/Spiritual Findings of Emanuel Swedenborg
By Wilson Van Dusen
A clinical psychologist's account of Swedenborg's inward journey, which resulted in strikingly modern writings about the psyche.

MY RELIGION
By Helen Keller
Helen Keller's inspiring personal account of Swedenborg's writings as a source of her own courage and strength.

THE HOLY CENTER
By Dorothea Harvey
A presentation of elements of Jewish ritual with ecumenical breadth and personal insight, as symbolic of contemorary spiritual values and processes.

Books by Emanuel Swedenborg

HEAVEN AND HELL
Swedenborg's revolutionary vision of the afterlife as an extension of the inner realities of the psyche.

ARCANA COELSTIA (HEAVENLY SECRETS) 12 volumes
A detailed analysis of the symbolic meanings of the books of Genesis and Exodus as guides to the unfoldment of human consciousness.

THE APOCALYPSE REVEALED 2 volumes
A similar analysis of the subtext of the enigmatic Book of Revelation, with particular emphasis on inner changes in the Christian church.

THE APOCALPYSE EXPLAINED 6 volumes
A comprehensive examination of most of the Book of Revelation, with copious references to other books of the Bible.

DIVINE LOVE AND WISDOM
A far-reaching philosophical/religious exploration of love as the basis of existence.

DIVINE PROVIDENCE
A sequel to the above, celebrating free will as an inherent principle of the divine master plan.

TRUE CHRISTIAN RELIGION
Swedenborg's own systematization of his theological writings into a unified vision of a new age with beliefs predicated on inner realities rather than outward forms.

JOURNAL OF DREAMS
With a Commentary by Wilson Van Dusen
Only recently available in English translation, Swedenborg's private dream journal reveals an eighteenth-century scientist struggling to interpret his own subconscious in a manner anticipating the work of Freud and Jung.

SPIRITUAL DIARY
Swedenborg's private diary, chronicling over twenty years of his visonary experiences.

THE ATHANASIAN CREED
A working MS exploring the relationship of Swedenborg's thought to early Christian doctrine.

CONJUGIAL LOVE
An extensive treatment of the implications of spiritual sexuality for earthly marriage.

THE LAST JUDGMENT (Posthumous)
A working MS on the subtext of Christian apocalyptic expectations.

THE NEW JERUSALEM AND ITS HEAVENLY DOCTRINE
A concise survey of the distinctive terminology of *Arcana Coelestia*.

A VIEW FROM WITHIN
Compiled and translated by George F. Dole
A Compendium of Swedenborg's Theological Thought in modern English.

See also:

THE UNIVERSAL HUMAN (A 1984 translation by Rev. George F. Dole, with preface by Dr. Stephen Larsen) New York, The Paulist Press, 1984. Excerpts from *Arcana Coelestia* on the symbolism of the human body; also includes Soul-Body Interaction (= Intercourse between the Soul and the Body), Swedenborg's most concise presentation of his cosmology.

Motion Pictures (Each available in 16mm, VHS, Beta, U-Matic, and other video formats)

SWEDENBORG: The Man Who Had To Know   30 minutes
Featuring Lillian Gish, narrated by Eddie Albert.
Award-winning television docu-drama about Swedenborg's life and writings, with a script exerpted from his books, journals, and other eighteenth-century accounts.

BLAKE: The Marriage of Heaven and Hell   30 minutes
Starring Anne Baxter and George Rose
Academy Award winner Anne Baxter and Tony Award winner George Rose recreate William Blake's inner world and artistic achievements, using Blake's own words, in this award-winning television docu-drama.

JOHNNY APPLESEED AND THE FRONTIER WITHIN   30 minutes
Starring veteran actor Joseph Davies and featuring Lillian Gish
This film explores the visionary side of John Chapman, 1774-1845, better known as Johnny Appleseed. It shows another aspect of the man who was a friend of the Indian and settler alike, a planter of appleseeds as well as the spiritual seeds of Emanuel Swedenborg.

IMAGES OF KNOWING   15 minutes

A highly acclaimed, award-winning, lyrical exploration of the processes of nature as reflections of the processes of mind, written by Rev. George F. Dole.

THE OTHER SIDE OF LIFE   30 minutes

Narrated by Tony Award winner George Rose.

People who have had near-death experiences testify to a radically different view of themselves as a result. This lyrical film coordinates text and images to introduce the viewer to the deathless side of human nature — ideal for both counselors and individuals. Written by the Rev. George F. Dole.